T0160121

DAUGHTER OF THE REICH

Also by Cindy Dowling:
Seachange: Australians in pursuit of the good life (Exisle 2004)

Daughter of the Reich

THE INCREDIBLE LIFE OF LOUISE FOX

LOUISE FOX AND CINDY DOWLING

Acknowledgements

I am grateful, as always, to my family for their patience
and perseverance. And, of course, many thanks to Louise
for her hospitality, her generosity and, most important, her
willingness to share the story of a most remarkable life.
Prost! – Cindy Dowling

First published 2006

Exisle Publishing Limited,
'Moonrising', Narone Creek Road, Wollombi, NSW 2325
www.exislepublishing.com

Copyright © Louise Fox and Cindy Dowling 2006
Louise Fox and Cindy Dowling assert the moral right to be identified as the
authors of this work.

All rights reserved. Except for short extracts for the purpose of review, no part of
this book may be reproduced, stored in a retrieval system or transmitted in any
form or by any means, whether electronic, mechanical, photocopying, recording or
otherwise, without prior written permission from the publisher.

Cataloguing-in-Publication Data
Fox, Louise, 1920- .
Daughter of the Reich : the incredible life of Louise Fox.

ISBN 0 908988 65 6

1. Fox, Louise, 1920- . 2. World War, 1939-1945 - Germany -
Biography. 3. Germans - Tasmania - Biography. 4. Germany
- Politics and government - 1933-1945. 5. Germany - Social
conditions - 1933-1945. I. Dowling, Cindy. II. Title.

940.548243

Designed and typeset by saso content & design pty ltd
Map by Fran Whild
Printed in China through Colorcraft, Hong Kong

1 3 5 7 9 10 8 6 4 2

CONTENTS

Prologue   7

1   The Approaching Storm   13

2   Under the Nazi Spell   38

3   Fighting Hitler's War   70

4   Hermann Goering's Secretary   100

5   A Terrible Defeat   127

6   The Aftermath of Madness   158

7   New Beginnings   189

Notes   215

Bibliography   220

Germany, showing the main places in Louise's story.

PROLOGUE

Does wisdom perhaps appear on the earth as a raven which is inspired by the smell of carrion?

Friedrich Nietzsche

SHE WAS WAITING FOR ME out in front of her nondescript Gold Coast apartment block, her body language portraying the kind of mild anxiety — or perhaps nervous excitement — most typically demonstrated by the very young and the very old.

As my taxi pulled away she came forward to shake my hand, and offered a tentative smile.

'Hello. I'm Louise Fox. Thank you for coming.' Her voice is warm, heavily accented and carries an undertone of caution. Meeting with me is a move into previously uncharted waters and she is not yet sure how the journey will end.

She was not quite what I had expected. Looking younger than her 85 years — with eyes of such a deep chocolate hue as to appear black, white hair cut into a fashionable bob, Roman nose set between delicate cheekbones — hers was a distinctive and decidedly atypical Germanic face.

'*The ideal Aryan is blond like Hitler, slim like Goering, well-built like Goebbels, masculine like Roehm.*' This was a popular catchphrase amongst critics of the Nazis in the early days of Adolf Hitler's leadership, satirising both the regime's absurd notion of Aryan perfection as well as its leaders' inability to match the standards they imposed on their countrymen.

Lacking the blue eyes, yellow hair and ruddy cheeks of the Aryan supermodel, Louise Fox had nevertheless been an exemplary soldier, a proud German and an obedient Nazi.

Later, when we know each other better, her dark features will become the subject of much good-natured bantering between the two of us.

'Lucky for you, Louise, that you had good German blood,' I teased her once during one of our many conversations. 'Otherwise you might have been in all sorts of trouble during the war.'

'I wouldn't have been here at all,' she replied, and both our smiles ended abruptly.

I follow her inside to a modest apartment that has that air of ordered calm so often found in the homes of those who live alone. A place for everything and everything in its place. Stuffed animals in rainbow shades dot the lounge room. Two impossibly fluffy creatures occupy strategic positions on the sofa, while on the floor below a troupe of monkeys, bears and cats stare out with glassy eyes to the pocket-handkerchief-sized rear garden beyond.

'My babies,' Louise explains with a hearty laugh when I ask about the animal collection. 'I collect them. And of course, now that people know I love them, they give them to me as presents.' She shrugs ruefully, as though her toy collection is something hopelessly beyond her control. 'They're in the bedroom too.'

One wall of the living area is dominated by a large bookcase housing an impressive row of books, their leather-bound black spines resplendent with gold lettering in Gothic type. The titles are in German, the only visible trace of Louise's homeland in the room.

She makes us both coffee, apologising that she only has instant to offer.

'I like to have good coffee, but it's too much for me to bother most of the time now. It takes too long to make, too much trouble just for one person.' Louise pauses for a moment, a 60-year-old memory surfacing as she stirs her drink. 'We used to make coffee so strong, you wouldn't believe it. Black coffee, very hot. We used to say it wasn't any good unless the spoon could stand up by itself.'

I ask how she slept after a day drinking such high-grade caffeine shots.

'We didn't sleep much. That was the idea. We were at war. The coffee kept us going. And that was the way our commanding officers insisted we make it.'

It is my first introduction to Louise's Fox's past — a minor yet telling insight into a life most remarkable.

I had flown to the Gold Coast at my publisher's behest to interview a woman described to me as Hermann Goering's secretary. Like many people, I had always had a fascination — albeit a fairly morbid one — with Nazism and Hitler. The Nazi reign in Germany was one of the most bizarre and horrific episodes in modern history — an unsettling mix of pure theatre and pure savagery. Who hasn't heard the dark tales of extermination camps or lampshades fashioned from human skin, or watched grainy footage of Hitler's manic oratory, the cheerful violence of the public book burnings or the eerie precision of the Reich's endless procession of child soldiers declaring their willingness to die for the Führer, and wondered if such Kafkaesque terrors could really have taken place in the heart of Europe a mere six decades ago?

The opportunity to speak at length with someone who had been a player on the mad stage of Nazi Germany — even one with a minor part — was intriguing and far too tempting to refuse.

My reasons for sitting in that sunny Gold Coast living room were self-serving and uncomplicated. But what of Louise's motives? Why would a woman who had obviously embraced a quiet, conservative existence, who seemed content to live out her remaining years in the sun, agree to expose herself as an active participant in one of history's most hated regimes?

'Because I think people need to know the truth,' is her unhesitatingly reply. As I would learn over the coming months, Louise Fox is a straight talker and not given to procrastination in word or deed. 'War, my dear, is a terrible, terrible thing. I know people don't need me to tell them that, but I do think that some people need to be reminded of the fact. In war, there are never any winners. Everyone suffers. People forget the reality of that, and that's why wars never end. People will always hurt one another because they forget the lessons of history, time and time again.'

Had she kept her Nazi links a secret in the past?

'Not a secret exactly ... but it is not something that you go around telling everyone. You choose who you can trust, who you can tell. Some people you might tell a little, a few you might tell more details. There are still people out there who are capable of being very nasty, who might want revenge. I've had people in the past refuse to speak to me when they find out I am German and was in the war. Now, of course, not so much. But I am concerned, yes, about how some people might react.'

Later, erring on the side of caution, we agree that she adopt the pseudonym Louise Fox for the purposes of this book.

Gingerly, I ask the inevitable question. Do you regret having been a Nazi?

It is then that I see the first signs of a steely resolve, an inner toughness that belies her little-old-lady exterior.

'I was not a Nazi by choice. Very few people in Germany were. The world has forgotten that. If you say you were a Nazi, people think you were a killer, a criminal. Hitler and the others, they were criminals, it is true. But ordinary Germans? We had no choice. Virtually everyone had to join the Nazi party — so really, we were all Nazis. We were the victims of a dictatorship. We had no idea of what was going on. We didn't want a war, we didn't know about the concentration camps, the mass killings. We were victims too of Hitler's madness. What was done in Germany's name was terrible. But I cannot personally feel guilty about it. I did not know. That is the truth. I hope you will believe me.'

There is a flash of genuine anger in her voice, and the sense that she has defended herself and her nation like this countless times before, in other rooms, before other inquisitors.

As I would soon come to realise, Louise Fox was far more than Hermann Goering's secretary. A feisty, fiercely intelligent woman, Louise was born in the same year that a moody Munich artist named Adolf Hitler joined the German Workers' Party, a fledgeling group of right-wing extremists he would soon rename the National Socialist Workers' Party, or Nazi Party for short.

Louise was 13 when Hitler assumed the Chancellorship of Germany, and for the next thirteen years became an adult in a society whose overriding purpose was to bring Hitler's crazed visions to fruition.

Hitler did more than lead Germany into the Second World War; he also infected an entire generation with his madness. Louise Fox was very much a product of the Hitler years. Coming into the world just as Hitler was rising to power, she was nursed on Nazi doctrine and spent her childhood surrounded by the mechanisms of Hitler's dogma — the Hitler Youth, the endless propaganda, the institutionalised racism, the shadowy secret police. Little wonder that when the time came, Louise joined the war effort with enthusiasm, fully accepting the righteousness of the German cause.

The day would arrive when Louise Fox and Adolf Hitler would finally meet face-to-face; a brief encounter, most likely immediately forgotten by one, and seared indelibly on the memory of the other. But even if Louise had never personally laid eyes on her Führer, he would remain perhaps the most significant individual in her life, just as he was for millions of her countrymen who endured both the Nazi reign and the terrible war that followed.

The little grey-haired woman who sat across the table from me had lived a life of incredible extremes and had watched and played her own small role in one of the most violent and momentous periods of world history.

What struck me most on the day of our very first meeting was the extraordinary stoicism that Louise had displayed throughout the myriad joys and tragedies of her life. The passage of time and an inherently German ability to be pragmatic and even reserved in the face of high emotion offered only a partial explanation.

But, as I would discover, what may appear to an outsider to be a kind of emotional remoteness, Louise regards as a hard-earned protective shell.

'War makes you hard. That can be a good thing and a bad thing. When you suffer a lot, you can either get weaker or stronger. I like to think it made me stronger. Either way, it changes you forever.'

Society is quick to create monsters. We like evil to be easily recognisable and clearly labelled. The methodical genocide carried out by the Nazis, as well as the millions of lives lost fighting the war they were hell-bent on starting, resulted from unmistakable acts of evil. And yet they were carried out by and in the name of very ordinary people, most of whom were unaware of the full extent of the savagery of their leaders.

Louise Fox was a loyal Nazi but she was no monster. Nor were millions of her countrymen. She was a young woman who loved clothes, makeup and parties — who would rather have spent her youth gossiping about boys and trying on shoes than fighting the Allies. Time, circumstance and Adolf Hitler made that an impossibility. History is played out by human beings — with all their countless foibles and failings. Like the truth, history is composed of myriad shades of grey and cannot be seen in simplistic shades of black and white, good and bad, right and wrong.

Louise Fox's journey from the shadows of fascism to the bright sunshine of the Queensland coast has been remarkable. An everyday woman thrust into the front row of history, her story is one of high adventure, of loss and despair and, ultimately, of the relentless battle between what the world teaches you and what you know to be right.

1 THE APPROACHING STORM

'Our fathers and ourselves sowed dragons' teeth. Our children know and suffer armed men.'

Stephen Benet, 'Litany for Dictatorships' *1936*.

PERCHED ON THE EDGE of the Baltic Sea in the far north of Germany lies the port town of Wismar. A thriving shipbuilding and commercial fishing centre, modern-day Wismar is also a popular haunt for tourists, drawing in day-trippers from both Germany and Denmark, a ferry ride away across Wismar Bay.

While the clumsy, Soviet-inspired concrete apartment blocks of the outlying suburbs don't let the visitor forget Wismar was once part of the former East Germany, the ancient town square is a picture-postcard kind of place, blessed with Gothic architecture, medieval shop fronts and stunning Baltic Sea vistas. The imposing 200-foot steeple of St Mary's Church — all that remains of a 13th century cathedral damaged by aerial bombers during World War II and deliberately destroyed by the Communist regime in 1960 — is a popular attraction. Film buffs may already be familiar with Wismar's old market square without even realising it — silent film director Friedrich Murnau used Wismar's winding alleyways as the backdrop to his classic vampire flick *Nosferatu*.

The UNESCO-listed site is a busy spot on a sunny day — bustling with tourists, all hoping to capture the essence of thousands of years of history with a couple of happy-snaps before moving on to Lübeck, Rostock, Stalsund or one of the other pretty towns that dot the well-travelled Baltic Coast road.

It was here in the German summer of 1920 — within strolling distance of the sea and the iron and salt tang of the busy port — that the modest apartment of Fritz and Lucy Fox was becoming an increasingly unhappy place. Despite being only six months married, the couple were coming to the realisation that their marriage had been a mistake. The stark differences between the two, which only a year before had seemed such a trifling, romantic irony, now seemed insurmountable.

Fritz was a talented classical musician just embarking on a promising career with the local symphony orchestra. A gentle, sensitive man, he shared with many creative types a propensity for indecision and a desire to avoid personal conflict at almost any cost. The contrast with his 20-year-old wife could not have been more marked. The daughter of a well-to-do factory owner, the former Miss Lucy Priestaff was fashionably plump and decidedly pragmatic — a tough-minded young woman with a booming voice and a frequently intimidating manner who desired a career of her own as an accountant.

A shy artist who often spoke in whispers and a strident, headstrong woman who preferred ambition to art, action to dreams — in the normal scheme of things such a romantic match would have revealed its truths long before they ever thought of walking down the aisle together. However, an unplanned pregnancy had suddenly changed the course of both their lives and made the unlikely match an inevitability.

While hedonistic Berlin (a city famously described as the urban equivalent of a 'highly desirable woman ... in lace underwear ...'[1] during the 1920s) would have easily forgiven such a moral lapse, the conservative, largely Protestant folk of Wismar would not. A wedding was simply the only course of action. Hurriedly and doubtless with some reluctance, the pair had become husband and wife.

The arrival of a daughter whom they duly called Louise saw dreams put on hold and ambitions reined in. Motherhood also saw Lucy's career plans seriously curtailed while Fritz, well intentioned but impractical and more suited to the orchestra pit than family life, was suddenly responsible for a wife and child he had not counted on.

Regret and disappointment, if left unchecked, are both poisons of a similar kind. Louise's earliest memories are of a modest two-bedroom apartment in a middle-class area of Wismar where recrimination and a pervasive sense of loss always hung in the air.

'The apartment was nothing very special in itself. Not a rich person's home, not a poor person's home. I guess we were average in terms of wealth, although I say that from an adult perspective, looking back in time. A child really has no notion of such things.

'I do recall though that, while we were certainly not rich, we had far more paintings and more expensive pieces of furniture than many of our neighbours. Both my parents were art and music lovers — one of the few things they had in common really — and the walls of our apartment were decorated with many paintings. Some of them might have been valuable — I really don't know. Most would have been wedding presents or gifts from my mother's parents — who were quite wealthy and knew how much my parents appreciated such gifts. We had some very nice vases too — big, decorative ones that I can remember dusting very, very carefully.

'We had some lovely pieces of furniture — carved chairs and such. Again, these were gifts from my grandparents. My grandfather owned a furniture manufacturing business. I remember that these pieces were carefully looked after — we knew they were special. I sometimes wonder whether being surrounded by those few, special objects as a very young child helped me to develop a love for fine things later on. I have always liked good quality — food, clothing, furniture. I have no time for rubbish, for cheap things. I would rather go without something than compromise with a poor quality version of it. Of course, there were times — thanks to Hitler and later thanks to bad luck — that I had no choice but to compromise and simply accept whatever I could get. It certainly went against my nature to do so.'

An active, high-spirited child with a shock of dark hair and a relentlessly inquisitive nature constantly stifled by her mother's short temper — 'I always wanted to know more about the world, I was always wanting to ask questions, but I knew that most of the time, I would just make my mother angry' — Louise's early years paint a bleak picture of family dysfunction.

'My parents were always arguing with one another about something. My mother usually won every argument — she was a very bossy woman and just shouted my father down until he gave in. My relationship with her was bad from the very beginning. My mother did not want a baby. She wanted my father at first, mind you, but not a child. Or at least not me. She was always cruel to me throughout my entire childhood and I do believe it was born out of resentment. She resented the position I had put her in. She resented having to care for me, having to stay home and look after me. From my mother I got orders, never love. I had a very unhappy childhood in that respect. And childhood is a very long time.

'What I remember most is my mother always yelling at me. She was so strict. I could do nothing right. She yelled at me to get out of bed in the morning, yelled at me to do the housework, yelled at me to go to bed. I was beaten quite regularly too, usually for little things. At first, I didn't understand why she treated me this way. I was quite bitter about it all for a very long time. Even as a very young girl I remember always feeling confused, scared and very resentful. Later of course, I learnt to simply accept what couldn't be changed. Now, it's all in the past I suppose. But a million years could never make me forget.'

Louise quickly learnt that her father would be no ally in her despair.

'My father was always much kinder to me, but he was a weak man in many ways. My mother was the strong one, always the boss. If he disagreed with her about anything, she just shouted him down. It was the same when she was abusing me. He didn't intervene. My father preferred to keep out of her way as much as he could. He preferred to keep his mouth shut whenever possible.

'My mother had a way of making people feel inadequate. I remember one day she went into a tirade at him because something in the apartment needed repairing. She was actually trembling with rage. Of course, he was a musician; he wasn't allowed to use tools in case he damaged his hands. She knew that, but she yelled at him anyway. He had no answer for her.'

While young Louise felt a relatively close bond with her father, his haplessness in the face of Lucy Fox's tirades at times tested both his daughter's love and her patience.

'There were times when I would have wished that he were stronger, that he would stand up to her. That he would stand up for me, I suppose. I probably resented him sometimes for his weakness, but what could I do? I was just a child, I had no power. I certainly can't ever recall begging him to help me. I think children just accept things as being the way life is. And times were different then too — men were perhaps not as involved with their children as they are these days. Most men of my father's generation simply left the raising of the children to their wives. And that's what my father did. I was well aware from a very early age that my mother wasn't fair or reasonable and that she didn't really love me. To be truthful, I don't think she even liked me very much. But I accepted it. And I knew that it was a problem I would have to bear mostly on my own.

'They were two people who should never have married in the first place. It wasn't a happy marriage and it wasn't a happy life. When my parents finally got a divorce after 25 years of marriage, all I could think of was what a terrible waste of time it had all been. What a tragedy it had been for all of us.'

But while the Fox family battled their own private demons, the world outside their front door was itself a place of relentless uncertainty and disorder.

The Western world had been utterly transformed by the awful magnitude of World War One. On the day of Germany's surrender on 9 November 1918, more than 8.5 million young men lay dead and 21 million more were wounded.[2] In France, an astonishing 11 per cent of the pre-war population had been killed or injured, in Great Britain that figure was eight percent.[3] Russia had suffered staggering casualties with more than 1.7 million dead soldiers; the Germans had lost almost two million.

Everywhere, proud cities and countless human lives lay in ruins. Economies that had been vibrant pre-1914 were now struggling, starved by four years of feeding the voracious appetite of war.

Of course, nowhere did the scars of war cut deeper than in Germany. Despite suffering three unsustainable defeats at Marne, the Somme and Verdun in the last months of 1918, news of their country's surrender came as a terrible shock to the average German citizen. Under the quasi-dictatorial regime of General Erich Ludendorff, the Quartermaster-General and the man charged with leading the war effort, media reporting of the conflict had been heavily censored. Defeats were ignored, victories wildly exaggerated. Every soldier's letter sent home from the front was carefully edited for any references to defeat or despair. In July 1918, the German Foreign Minister, Admiral Paul von Hintze, refused to release details of the calamitous losses at Marne, declaring censorship necessary to 'nurse the patriotic feelings of the German people'.[4]

As late as September 1918, some Berlin newspapers were delirious with the news that Germany had won the war.

On the day the armistice was signed, Adolf Hitler — then a corporal in the army — was in hospital recovering from the effects of a mustard gas attack sustained in battle with British forces in France.

Temporarily blinded as a side-effect of the gas, Hitler's reaction to the news of the German surrender is graphically — and rather melodramatically — recalled in *Mein Kampf*.

> And so it had all been in vain. In vain all the sacrifices and privations; in vain the hunger and thirst of months which were often endless ... in vain the death of two million who died. Had they died for this, the soldiers of August and September, 1914? Did all this happen only so that a gang of wretched criminals could lay hands on the Fatherland?[5]

Hitler was not a man often accused of understatement. Nonetheless, there is no reason to disbelieve the depth of feeling in this particular account, or to doubt that it was a view shared by millions of his countrymen.

This particular passage is also interesting in its description of the 'wretched criminals' responsible for the German defeat. Within days of the surrender, many high-ranking military officials and a handful of opportunistic politicians had actively begun to circulate the so-called 'Stab in the Back' theory. This suggested that the real cause for Germany's defeat was a betrayal from within by various minority groups, including the Communists, the Republicans, the Jews, the gypsies and assorted foreigners — all aided by unscrupulous businessmen eager to profit from war and politicians too incompetent to stop them. These outsiders, the theory went, had secretly and actively worked towards ensuring an Allied victory by siphoning money away from the war effort and into their own pockets, and by continuously disrupting the political and social agenda at a time when the entire country should have been united in the war effort.

It was a spurious and obviously self-serving piece of propaganda without any basis in fact. But for a nation unable to accept defeat, it proved to be a most welcome lie. The term 'November criminals' —

referring both to those who signed the Armistice and those now blamed for having instigated it — rapidly entered the lexicon.

By 1925, when *Mein Kampf* was first published, the lie had become an indisputable fact. Recounting a period in 1917 when he had been wounded and sent from the front to a city-based battalion to recover, Hitler was in no doubt as to who was really responsible for his nation's failure.

> The offices were filled with Jews. Nearly every clerk was a Jew and nearly every Jew was a clerk. I was amazed at this plethora of warriors of the chosen people and could not help but compare them with their rare representatives at the Front.
>
> As regards economic life, things were even worse. Here the Jewish people had become really 'indispensable'. The spider was slowly beginning to suck the blood out of the people's pores. Through the war corporations, they had found an instrument with which, little by little, to finish off the national free economy. Thus, in the year 1917, nearly the whole of production was under the control of Jewish finance.[6]

With the declaration of surrender came the news that the ruling royal house of the Hohenzollerns — along with the numerous minor regional kings that made up Germany's convoluted monarchy — was to be disbanded and replaced by a republic. For the first time in its history, Germany would become a democracy. While Kaiser Wilhelm II had not been universally loved, his forced abdication would be held up by detractors as yet another instance of German submission to the Allies, and to long-held British and French concerns about Germany's dictatorial political structure.

The dismissal of the Kaiser created a political vacuum which disgruntled elements from both the left and right factions of German politics rushed to fill. Socialist groups, long a significant force in

German politics and one of the few factions that had publicly and vehemently opposed the war, suddenly found their numbers swelled by thousands of disillusioned soldiers returning from the Front. Armed uprisings led by demobilised soldiers and sailors began to occur throughout Germany with the speed and unpredictability of brush-fires. Inspired by the Bolshevik revolution, supporters of organisations like the USPD (Unabhängige Sozialdemokratische Partei Deutschlands or Independent Social Democrats) took to the streets of Berlin and Munich in ever-increasing numbers, encouraging general strikes and demanding nothing less than the formation of a Soviet-style republic.

In response, right-wing groups, fearing a successful Communist takeover, decided to fight fire with fire. A motley collection of anti-Bolshevik troops was quickly assembled, most notably from the ill-disciplined rabble of the Freikorps (literally the volunteer corps) and segments of the German Army. At its peak, the battle between these opposing forces was akin to a civil war. The conflict reached its zenith in January 1919 when an extreme left faction of the USPD, known as the Spartakus and led by Karl Leibknecht and the Jewish revolutionary Rosa Luxemburg, occupied key civic and government buildings in Berlin for five days and called on every worker to join them in overthrowing the status quo. Few took up that challenge — hardly surprising given that choosing any side, left or right, carried a very high risk of personal injury, and the Army eventually killed the uprising's leaders and key followers. Spring 1919 would reveal dozens of battered corpses emerging from the fast-thawing waters of Berlin's canals.

Four days after Leibknecht and Luxemburg were beaten to death in a Berlin alley, National Assembly elections for the new republican government were held. The vote proved to a be great success for more moderate political forces, with the USPD and its counterparts resoundly defeated in most states.

The new government, known as the Weimar Republic after the · town where its constitution was formulated, was based on a semi-presidential system supported by a Reichstag (or parliament) elected through a system of proportional representation. Friedrich Ebert, leader of the centrist Majority Social Democrats (or MSPD), was named as president.

It is obvious that the Weimar government was hopelessly compromised from the start. Despite an often admirable policy agenda, which formally legislated concepts such as universal suffrage and workers' rights while implementing a comprehensive public welfare system, in the poisonous atmosphere of the day, good intentions were never going to be enough. It remained a hastily convened alternative, conceived during the aftershock of war and determined with the gun of revolution held to its head. It pleased few and enraged many while achieving the rare trick of alienating both left- and right-wing extremists.

Any possibility that Weimar could have eventually extracted itself from the impenetrable web of opposition surrounding it was permanently put to rest in June 1919 with the signing of the Treaty of Versailles. Amid the unrivalled splendour of the Bourbons' last — and most excessive — country retreat, the German peace delegation agreed to a raft of conditions that would send shockwaves through all levels of German society.

Germany lost significant tracts of territory (including the coal-rich Saar), the right to an air force and had its army restricted to a mere 100,000 men. Most intolerable for the German people however was Clause 231 — the infamous war guilt clause — which stated that Germany took full responsibility for all loss of life and property incurred during the four years of fighting. To admit guilt was to admit liability and Germany was required to pay war reparations in the amount of 269 billion gold marks. This was a mind-boggling debt for any nation, let along one that was already teetering on the financial brink.

The old imperial government's reckless funding of the war had created significant inflation. In 1919, the German mark was worth less than 30 per cent of its pre-war value. Under the terms of Versailles, Germany had lost some 12 per cent of its territory, 10 per cent of its population, 15 per cent of its arable land, 75 per cent of its iron production, 68 per cent of its zinc ore resources and 26 per cent of its coalfields.[7] With its currency in a dangerous cycle of fluctuation and its capacity to earn severely curtailed, the nation's ability to pay this international debt was doubtful from the outset. Despite the reparations bill being reduced to 132 billion gold marks in 1921, German outrage at the perceived unfairness of the demands continued to fester.

At Versailles, the French Prime Minister George Clemenceau's bitter prophecy that in victory they would 'squeeze the German lemon till the pip squeaks' came to pass. To those on the receiving end of the Allies' revenge, the treaty soon came to be referred to scornfully as 'das Diktat' — the dictation.

The lead story of the *Illustrated London News* of 28 June 1919 reported on mass demonstrations in Berlin and other German cities against the signing. It also quoted the right-leaning and widely respected German Field-Marshal Paul von Hindenburg addressing one gathering with these fiery and defiant words:

> God does not desert us. We must take care that the great work of Wilhelm I and Bismarck is not crushed to pieces. Germany ... will rise again. This is my firm belief and I can only beg you to think in this sense and, when the hour strikes, also to act.[8]

He was not the only high-ranking soldier to see the folly of Versailles. His French counterpart, the commander of Allied forces on the western front, General Ferdinand Foch, put it even more succinctly. 'This is not a peace treaty,' he said. 'It is an armistice for 20 years.'[9]

WISMAR IN THE YEAR of Louise's birth was a far from typical German town. To begin with, it had only been officially part of Germany for some 17 years. In the period 1648–1903, Wismar had been under the direct rule of Sweden and was reclaimed only after the Swedes demanded — and received — the princely sum of 1,258,000 riksdalers (a now-extinct Swedish currency) to relinquish control.

Prior to Swedish rule, the town had also formed part of the once-powerful Hanseatic League — a loose collection of port towns and cities in northern Germany, Poland, the Netherlands and Latvia that combined their trading and military strength from the 10th to the late 16th centuries to the mutual benefit of all. Sailors, traders and artisans from all over Europe were regular and welcome visitors to these self-proclaimed 'free towns', bringing with them their languages, cultures and differing world views. Geographically, Wismar is far closer to Denmark than to Berlin — the lights of the Danish coast are clearly visible from the shores of Wismar Bay — and like much of regional Germany at the time, had always placed local concerns well ahead of any directives emanating from Munich or the capital.

Sun, sea, history and distance may have created a certain political apathy in Wismar, but even in this most atypical part of the Fatherland, the ramifications of Versailles were inescapable.

In July 1914, prior to the outbreak of war, there were 4.2 deutschmarks to the US dollar. By July 1919, that rate had risen to 14 marks to the dollar, largely due to the cost of funding the war effort. The following July, the exchange rate had blown out to 39.5 and by July 1921, it had reached a crippling 76.7 marks to the dollar.[10] The German economy, already on shaky foundations before 1918, simply could not support the added weight of reparations repayments.

Desperate to halt the currency decline, the Republic opted to default on its debt. By way of response, France and Belgium (the two nations most financially devastated by the war with Germany and with the claim to the biggest slice of the Versailles pie) invaded the Ruhr region, Germany's industrial heart, and took control of the valuable mining and manufacturing bases it contained. Rather than work under foreign masters — and with the active encouragement of the Ebert government — workers began a series of rolling stoppages and walkouts, which in turn put more pressure on the German economy and left the Republic with little choice but to pay the strikers' wages.

The crisis swept the currency into a hyperinflationary spiral, sending the real value of salaries and savings plummeting. As a solution, the Weimar government simply printed more currency, which had the effect of devaluing the mark even further. By mid-1923, one American dollar was the equivalent of 4,620,455 marks. The German currency was virtually worthless. The madness peaked in November 1923 when the exchange rate stood at an astonishing 4,200,000,000,000 (trillion) to one.[11] Shortly after, reparations payments were resumed.

The social fallout of hyperinflation was enormous. A nation that had endured terrible food shortages for several years now found that, even with more food available, they could no longer afford to buy it. Workers were paid in hundred million and, later, billion mark notes. A wheelbarrow stuffed with near-useless money was required to buy a single loaf of bread. Money was used instead of kindling to fire wood stoves — it was more economical to burn the currency than to use it to purchase wood. The poor began to show signs of malnutrition. The middle class staved off the worst of the hunger by selling possessions — jewellery, furniture, evening clothing. In Berlin and Munich there were reports of angry housewives attacking storeowners — and quite often one another — in response to food prices. Workers were paid up to three times a day in an attempt to counter the constant changes in currency values.

Judging from this recollection by Konrad Heiden, the distinguished anti-fascist author of *Der Fuehrer* and a Nazi contemporary, such schemes served little purpose.

They dashed to the nearest food store, where a line was already formed. Again they moved slowly, oh how slowly, forward. When you reached the store a pound of sugar might have been obtainable for two million marks, but by the time you had come to the counter, all you could buy was half a pound and the sales-women would say the price had gone up again. With the millions or billions you bought sardines, sausages, sugar, perhaps even a little butter, but as a rule the cheaper margarine — always things that would keep for a week, until next payday, until the next stage in the fall of the market ...[12]

The New York Times of 30 October 1923 illustrates the absurdity of the German financial crisis.

An American entered a Berlin restaurant and asked for all the food an American dollar would buy.

Soup, several meat dishes, fruit and coffee were served. While the guest was smoking his cigar the waiter brought another plate of soup and later, another meat dish.

'What does this mean?' the astonished and satisfied guest asked.

The waiter bowed politely and replied: 'The dollar has gone up again'.[13]

Her youth allowed Louise to remain oblivious to much of the extreme hardship that almost every German family, including her own, bore during the years of hyperinflation.

'I don't ever remember being extremely hungry as a young child, but I did have a sense that food was scarce and always very valuable. We ate potatoes and vegetables mostly, with meat only very occasionally. Of course later, during the war, meat became almost impossible to find and the food shortages were far worse. My father always worked and, even with the mark plummeting, I believe we were better off than many others. We were an average income family, not rich but not poor either. So, we managed.

'My father's parents lived on one of the large rural estates in Mecklenburg-Schwerin: my grandfather was a supervisor there — and they would sometimes send us food parcels.

'As I got older, I gradually became aware that many people in Wismar were extremely poor and that unemployment in the town was always high. No one was really happy back then. People went from day to day, just hoping that tomorrow might be better. Every day there was concern that tomorrow there might not be enough to eat or there might not be a job to go to. I understood, even at a young age, that times were hard, but of course a child doesn't dwell on such matters very long.'

But many others did dwell on their continued misfortune. Empty stomachs and empty pockets gradually began to focus the German people's minds on the need for political reform in a way that neither the November revolution nor the new Republic had been able to. It is no coincidence that Hitler and the Nazi Party first came to national prominence in November 1923 — at the very peak of hyperinflation — with a failed attempt to seize control from the government through armed intervention.

In truth, Hitler's Beer Hall Putsch (so called because it began with three key figures of the Republic being held hostage by the Nazis in a Munich beer cellar) was a rather naïve attempt at revolution: hastily organised, undermanned and always doomed to failure. Nonetheless, it was viewed by many as a desperate response to desperate times, although as *The New York Times* reported, the Nazis were still a long way from capturing the Zeitgeist of popular discontent.

> Munich experienced little of the putsch and the rest of Bavaria failed to react to it. In Berlin, it provoked a minimum of interest and no alarm ... the populace generally appears to be taking very little interest in the affair, being much more concerned with the increasing price of food.[14]

For little Louise, the uncertainty of the mark paled into insignificance beside the ever-present tension that existed between mother and daughter. By the age of four, the sour, destructive bond between Louise and Lucy had etched itself on the little girl's general demeanour. The energetic, determined child with a million questions and an enormous appetite for life had been forced into the background. In her place, a quiet, frequently sullen girl emerged, a child who found the solution to the conflict between her mother's endless demands and her own free-spirited yearnings in deceit.

'I became a naughty child. I was defiant and I liked to argue the point with people. I was always telling lies, often for no reason. I would tell stories to other children in the neighbourhood, silly stories that I thought made me seem more interesting. Or I would tell my mother I had swept the floor, when it was quite obvious I hadn't. I wasn't a good liar at first, although I got better at it over the years. But when I first began to be deceptive, I got caught out nearly all the time. And of course, it just made my mother dislike me more and made her treat me even more harshly. I was giving her an excuse really. I have no idea why I started acting this way. But that's what happens when you don't get love. It changes you.'

The arrival of a little sister in 1924 only exacerbated the antipathy between the two.

'From the day my sister Gerda was born she was always the obvious favourite. I remember overhearing my mother one day saying something nice about the baby, and me feeling sad. I don't know whether I was capable then of wondering why she was so pleased to be having another child when she didn't seem able to tolerate the one she already had, but at some level I suppose that was what I was feeling. Once Gerda was older, I thought my mother might start treating her in the same way she dealt with me. But it never happened.

'Gerda was always more talented, smarter, prettier than me. That wasn't Gerda's fault of course, but still, it was another cause for resentment and I think in some ways it did affect our relationship as sisters when we were growing up. We were not very alike anyway — we both loved music, but Gerda had more talent than me, she had played music all her life and even played professionally in jazz bands in France. I was always aware that my mother thought Gerda special. Me, she just didn't like.'

While Gerda toddled around the apartment basking in her mother's affection, Louise found herself with a new role — that of housekeeper.

'My mother was never a good housekeeper. She was not really interested in cleaning or cooking. She wanted to work in an office and have a housekeeper do all the domestic duties for her, but she couldn't because of her children. So, instead she decided I should start doing most of the housework. Apart from the yelling and her harshness, cleaning is the thing I remember most from my early childhood. As soon as I was old enough to hold a broom and dust a table, she had me doing it. And not just a little bit either. I would spend hours cleaning that apartment. Floors, windows, toilet.

'My mother was particularly fussy about clean floors. Especially the corners. She would have me mop the floor, and then come to check that I'd done a good job. She would always get down and look very closely at the corners. If they weren't right, she'd usually give me a slap, or sometimes a full beating, and then have me do the job until she judged it to be right. I often think she wasn't really happy until she had found something to criticise me for — she enjoyed punishing me, I'm sure.'

As Louise became older, the intensity of her mother's physical violence towards her escalated. Slaps were frequent and prolonged beatings not uncommon. On occasions, Lucy Fox's aggression went one dark step further and lapsed into ugly sadism.

'If my mother hated cleaning, she hated cooking even more. However, for a few years at least, I was still too young to operate the stove, peel the vegetables and so forth. So my mother had no choice but to cook for us, at least until I was old enough to take over.

'As with everything that she disliked, my mother was a terrible cook. I don't know whether she genuinely couldn't cook, or whether she was simply so disinterested in it that she put no effort into the task. Whatever her reasons, her meals were awful. At times they were simply inedible. Vegetables either overcooked or undercooked, meat raw or burnt, nothing with any seasoning or flavour. More than once, my father would look at his plate of food and simply pick it up, uneaten, and return it to the kitchen. If he ever complained about her cooking though, I didn't hear it.

'Unfortunately for me, I wasn't permitted to simply not eat her foul meals. She insisted I eat everything on my plate at every single meal. This one particular day the meal was either especially bad, or I was feeling more rebellious than usual. I ate some of it, but then told her I simply couldn't eat any more. It was making me feel sick. She yelled at me to finish every mouthful, and I started crying, and telling her I couldn't.

'Suddenly, she hit me a few times and then dragged me down into the basement of our apartment. It was dark and dirty down there, terrifying for a small child. There were mice. I could hear them scuttling around. She forced me into the basement, put the plate of uneaten food beside me and told me that I would stay down there in the dark until I had eaten everything. It was the most horrible feeling. I felt lost and I was scared of the dark. And I knew that my mother wouldn't change her mind — she would make me stay in that basement until her horrible meal was finished.'

Fighting back sobs and nausea, and trying to ignore a child's natural fear of what unknown creatures might lie in waiting in the basement's gloom, Louise slowly and painfully began to eat.

'The meal had gone stone cold by this time, which only made it worse. It seemed to take forever to eat — it went down my throat like lumps of cement. It was horrible. I kept gagging and feeling like I wanted to vomit, and I knew I had to fight that impulse. Finally, my plate was clean. I called for my mother and after a while she came stomping down the basement steps. But just as she took the plate away, my stomach knotted up and I couldn't help myself — I threw up everything all over the floor. The whole meal.'

Enraged all over again, Lucy Fox attacked her young daughter, beating her around the head and torso so hard that the bruises would remain for days after.

'When she had finished hitting me, she bought me a mop and bucket and made me clean up my vomit. And that was the end of the matter for her. For me though, it is something I have never forgotten my whole life.'

WHILE AN UNHAPPY MARRIAGE and a deficit of maternal instinct may have had a large role to play in Lucy Fox's abuse of her daughter, Louise believes that there were probably greater unknown forces at work.

'My mother was unhappy of course, but lots of people are unhappy. They don't all go around behaving as she did. I think her unhappiness was deeper than most, perhaps depression, perhaps even some type of mental illness. Such things were not really understood back then.'

It would be decades after the incident in the basement before Louise would finally discover the full extent of her mother's overwhelming despair.

'After the war my mother told Gerda about how unhappy she had been when we all lived as a family. This was the sort of thing she would only ever have told Gerda. She and I rarely discussed anything on a personal level. She confessed to Gerda that, prior to the start of the war, she had secretly purchased some shares in the hope that the price would rise and she would make enough money to leave us all behind.

Unfortunately for her, the shares lost money and she was stuck with us. Can you imagine a woman who could plan such a thing? It is one thing to leave your husband, but she was thinking of this while Gerda and I were still very young. She had no heart. There was something wrong with her. Perhaps I should feel sorry for her, but I can't. There are too many memories of her barking voice, of her hitting me around the head. I can't forgive that.'

Amidst so much unhappiness, Louise sought eager sanctuary in the fleeting moments of joy and the rare reassurance that came her way. Her father's great love — music — quickly became a treasured companion for his daughter too.

'I grew up with the sounds of my father's music always around me. He was a wonderful musician who could turn his hand to any instrument — he played clarinet, saxophone, cello, violin, piano.

'I was seven years old when I went to my first symphony concert. It was a magical thing for me, something unforgettable. Sitting in the dark, listening to the orchestra ... I could forget every-thing else for a little while. That love of music has stayed with me all these years, through everything that has happened — the good and the bad. I have always been very grateful for that aspect of my upbringing. Music lessons, art, literature — they are all gifts. We were lucky to have access to them from an early age. Gerda always showed much more promise than me as a musician of course, but that was okay. I just enjoyed playing and listening to beautiful sounds.'

Her maternal grandparents were another regular source of comfort. Ludwig and Minna Priestaff enjoyed a relatively privileged standard of living; Ludwig was a self-made businessman and well-regarded local figure and the couple were one of the few in Wismar able to afford their own home — a two-storey detached residence within walking distance of the Fox apartment. Both Louise and her mother were frequent visitors.

'I spent as much time there as I could, often overnight. My grand-parents were always very diplomatic about my mother. They were never critical of her in front of me, but they knew what she was like. My mother visited them very often too, usually to complain about my father. They never criticised him, either. 'You wanted the man and you got him. Now you have to live with him,' my grandmother used to say to her. They were lovely people and I was very close to them.

'I'm sure they didn't know how badly my mother treated me. They never asked, and I never told them, although I probably made it clear we weren't close. I think even they knew that my mother was a difficult person. It was a great comfort to me — knowing that my grandparents were kind and that I could go there so often. It made me feel a little safer somehow.'

People, including children, tend to have either one of two distinct reactions to adversity — there are those who submit to it and reconcile themselves to the situation, while others opt to confront and defy. Either way, the wounds of such intense and prolonged emotional abuse during her formative years could not have failed to leave permanent scars on Lucy's psyche. It occurred to me that the cruel lessons learnt during her stormy relationship with her mother may have played a part in toughening her resolve and enabled her to survive the even greater mental trauma of World War Two.

'It may have played a part my dear, it is hard to say. I suppose I am a strong-willed person. I don't suffer fools. I have always known who I like and who I don't. I have been through a great deal and always managed to cope somehow. Whether my childhood had anything to do with it or not, I don't know. It's also true that when terrible things happen in your life — especially something on such a large scale as Hitler and the war — what else can you do but cope? You can't simply roll over and die. Life must go on — regardless. That is part of what it is to be human.

'I can say that I had an inferiority complex until I was in my forties. Ridiculous really, but there you have it. I blame my mother for that. Even though I may have seemed confident and outgoing, I really wasn't. I spent many years not feeling good enough, of feeling like everyone else was somehow superior to me. I'm sure that being bullied the way I was caused those feelings. If someone says you are stupid and useless often enough, you start believing it must be true.'

At the age of six Louise commenced her education at the local elementary school in Wismar. Delighted to be free of her mother's controlling presence for at least a few hours each day, Louise flourished amidst the friendships and relative freedoms the schoolyard offered. Although not a particularly disciplined child — her rebellious instincts having followed her from home — the Louise of the schoolyard was a far cry from the chastened, shy child her mother had created. Having realised that the rules of her home life did not apply to the schoolyard, a more outgoing and happy Louise soon re-emerged, at least from 8.00 am to 1.00 pm each day when school was in session. She made friends with surprising ease, although the underlying need to please and to be accepted remained. Boys interested her far more than girls: 'I was a wild child and the girls were simply not wild enough for me.' And while she preferred sports to more academic pursuits, her natural intellect saw her usually hovering near the top of the class.

'I was quite good at school academically, I enjoyed learning. I still do today. When you stop learning you may as well be dead. I loved history best of all, and I enjoyed learning other languages. I was good at English, which proved to be a very useful skill later on in my life. Geography I enjoyed as well. When I look back it seems the subjects I liked best were those that somehow taught me about the world. Even then, I was interested in other places, exploring other countries. The only subject I was not good at was numbers, mathematics. I was terrible at that. It didn't interest me at all. And any type of sports, that was my real passion — running, jumping, hiking and swimming. I loved them all. I suppose I was a tomboy when I was little, although that changed when I got older.'

The friendships forged at school naturally spilled over into her limited leisure time, something that quickly disgruntled her mother.

'I had quite a few friends, mostly children I went to school with or those who lived around the area of our apartment. I was a fairly social child by this time and, of course, I was always keen to go and visit others since it gave me an excuse to get out of my own house for a while. I can remember spending quite a bit of time with a boy who lived next door, Hanse his name was. We were good friends for several years; we'd known each other all our lives really.

'I would walk to my friend's apartment after school or at weekends and we would play. At first, my mother was happy with that, provided I still got all my homework and all the cleaning done. But after a while, she started to resent it. She never really clearly told me why, but she seemed to like to have me around as much as possible. And she was always nervous about me going out in larger groups with my friends. So, sometimes she forbade me to go out and other times I just lied about what I was doing. I would tell her I had to go to a friend's house to study, and in fact would meet up with a group of other friends. We were just children, there was no harm being done and nobody else's parents seemed to mind. Even in this, my mother could not let me be.

'When I became a teenager, the situation just became worse. She did not trust me at all. When my other friends started to go to the movies together or meet somewhere for a meal, my mother often would not allow me to go with them. Usually, I had no money either of course, and she would rarely give me any. She kept me under very tight control — or at least she tried to. In reality, by the time I was thirteen, I had worked out how to sneak around and have at least a little bit of fun occasionally behind her back.'

FOR THE NEXT FEW YEARS Louise's life fell into a predictable if uneasy pattern between the steady rhythms of school and the jagged emotional peaks and troughs of family life. Outside the Fox's front door, Germany continued its slide into economic and social chaos. The country's economy had survived the assault of hyperinflation, only to be confronted in 1929 by an even greater challenge with the advent of the Great Depression. The political divide between left- and right-wing forces had also continued relatively unabated, and indeed both sides had become increasingly radicalised throughout the 1920s — partly in response to the gravity of Germany's predicament, but also largely because of the Weimar Republic's endless equivocation and contradictory approach to confronting its opponents.

Berlin and Munich and, increasingly, Germany's northern states were hotbeds of discontent, but in the Fox household politics remained an issue of only marginal interest.

'My parents were not political people. There didn't sit around the dinner table discussing the economy or the government a great deal. They had enough problems of their own to deal with, but that wasn't the only reason. I don't think that the average person in Wismar at that time was very interested in politics either — what they were concerned about was finding a job or making more money.

'Of course, I remember my mother and father talking about rations and food shortages and sometimes about the unemployment crisis, but they never expressed strong support for one political group or another. Like most Germans, they just wanted things to get better. Perhaps everyone should have talked about politics more in those days, thought about things more. Because, later, when everything changed and people suddenly wanted to have some say about what was happening in Germany, it was too late. We were no longer free to speak our minds.'

During the election campaign of 1932, Hitler paid a rare visit to the Baltic Coast. Now the undisputed leader of a formidable political force with an estimated membership of more than 800,000, he was scheduled to address a rally in the city of Lübeck, Wismar's near neighbour and another like-minded former member of the Hanseatic League. The good folk of Lübeck had other ideas. Outraged at his racial agenda, the regular violence inflicted by his SS troops on their political opponents and his threat to strip Hanseatic towns of small privileges such as flying their own flag, the mayor of Lübeck forbade Hitler to speak in the town. The rising political star was forced to speak instead in the tiny village of Bad Schwartau, which lay on the outskirts of Lübeck. Hitler would later portray this rare humiliation in the best possible light by insisting that Lübeck was a 'small city close to Bad Schwartau'.[15]

Lübeck's defiance had all the hallmarks of the region's old independence. But it was to be no more than a parting shot fired into the encroaching darkness.

Despite their rich maritime history, the northern states of Mecklenburg-Schwerin (which includes Wismar), Schleswig-Holstein and Oldenburg were predominantly rural areas, while the regional cities such as Kiel and Lübeck with their ports and strong manufacturing base, all had large working-class populations. Blue collar workers and peasant farmers were the two groups that had suffered most from both hyperinflation and the Great Depression.

In 1927 German manufacturing had been at a postwar high, and largely due to the necessity of making reparations payments, the country was emerging as one of Europe's most dynamic exporters. By 1930 however, thanks to the Wall Street collapse, manufacturing output had dropped 17 per cent and was still in free fall. By 1932, official employment figures showed that over five million Germans, around 30 per cent of the population, were without a job.[16]

At the elections in November of that year, more than 40 per cent of the population of Lübeck voted for the Nazi Party.[17] Over 30 per cent of the population of Wismar did the same. Northern Germany had become a Nazi stronghold.

Within two months Adolf Hitler would be named Chancellor of Germany and little Louise Fox's world would never be the same again.

2 UNDER THE NAZI SPELL

Violent, masterful, unafraid, cruel youth is
what I want. There must be nothing weak
and tender about them. The free, magnificent
predator must flash from their eyes again.
Thus will I wipe out thousands of years of
human domestication. Thus will I see before
me the noble raw material of nature.
— *Adolf Hitler*

THERE IS NOTHING POPULAR CULTURE abhors more than ambiguity.
Such is the enormous and pervasive influence of the media on our
collective consciousness, that even 60 years after the end of the Second
World War, even the mildest suggestion that Adolf Hitler made some
positive contribution to society can seem confronting. Ranked above
even Stalin, Mussolini and Pol Pot as the ultimate political demon, the
notion that Hitler might have been anything other than purposeful
evil incarnate is provocative.

'The thing that nobody ever mentions about Hitler was that he
was legitimately voted into power. He did not start out as a dictator.
He made the German people a lot of promises and he kept them. Until
he decided to start a war, he was doing a lot of good for the country.'

It's a view that Louise Fox makes no apologies for.

'When Hitler came to power there were millions of people out of
work. The French army had invaded the Ruhr and the reparations
were crippling everyone. No one in Germany was really happy. People

went from one day to the next wondering what they would eat today or whether they would have a job tomorrow. That is no way for anyone to live their lives and in Germany, an entire country was trying to exist that way. The elevation of Hitler wasn't really about politics — not for the average person, anyway — it was about hope, about finding someone who could help us out of the mess.

'And at first, he did help us. He reduced unemployment, he built the autobahns and when he got the French out of the Ruhr, he was a national hero. Nobody knew he wanted to start a war. Nobody knew that he would try to kill all the Jews. And by the time we did, it was too late to stop him. I know that a lot of people don't like to hear things like that these days. But it is the truth. And there is no point in hiding from the truth.'

Equally true is that the world of Louise's teenage years — that often turbulent but critical period during which the child becomes an adult and opinions, allegiances and political instincts are as malleable as putty — was one dominated in every facet by the presence of the Führer.

One of Hitler's first priorities on assuming power had been to commence implementation of a policy he called Gleichschaltung, or Nazification of the entire German population. The concept was both simple and breathtaking in its sheer scope and audacity. Hitler envisioned a nation where only Nazi ideology would be tolerated, where only Nazi viewpoints would be espoused and which, over time, could give rise to a race of people willing to docilely accept even the most extreme facets of his agenda.

Under the direction of his Propaganda Minister, the rabidly anti-Semitic Joseph Goebbels, Gleichschaltung was soon casting a shadow over every aspect of German social and economic life, from the blatant quashing of opposition political parties to the shamelessly reverential newspaper and radio reports produced by a cowed media.

The effects were immediate. William Shirer, in his definitive *Rise and Fall of the Third Reich*, offers the following insight:

No one who has not lived for years in a totalitarian land can possibly conceive how difficult it is to escape the dread consequences of a regime's calculated and incessant propaganda. Often in a German home or office or sometimes in a casual conversation with a stranger in a restaurant, a beer hall, a café, I would meet with the most outlandish assertions from seemingly educated and intelligent persons. It was obvious they were parroting some piece of nonsense they had heard on the radio or read in the newspapers. Sometimes one was tempted to say as much, but on such occasions one was met with such a state of incredulity, such a shock of silence, as if one had blasphemed their Almighty, that one realised how useless it was even to try to make contact with a mind which had become warped and for whom the facts of life had become what Hitler and Goebbels, with their cynical disregard for truth, said they were.[1]

Louise Fox was thirteen years old when Hitler became Chancellor. It was at school that she first recalls hearing his name mentioned and within months of the 1932 Reichstag elections, his image gazed down at her from the classroom wall.

'I cannot consciously remember the first day that Hitler's portraits were put up on the walls, or when we all started leaning about the Nazi Party. It seems sometimes like they were always there, but of course, that was not so. What 13-year-old gives much thought to a portrait hanging on the classroom wall?'

Even had the children wondered about the sudden emphasis on the new Chancellor in their studies, they would have been highly unlikely to query their teachers on the matter. Even prior to Nazi control, the German education system valued pupil discipline and obedience very highly. Teachers were largely rigid and authoritarian in their approach to their students, while the students themselves generally learned quickly that any form of defiance — even a simple question — usually resulted in some form of corporal punishment.

'Our teachers were very strict — I suppose we were always a little bit afraid of them. In those days, teachers were expected to be a little frightening — that was the way the children were kept under control. Talking in class was absolutely forbidden unless you were asked a question. If you spoke otherwise and were caught, you would often get the cane across your palm or your backside. Occasionally, the teachers would even hit the children with their bare hands — it was not considered the wrong thing to do back then.'

Louise herself felt the sting of the cane on more than one occasion, although she never felt any lasting resentment at either the severity of the punishment or towards the teacher handing it out.

'Oh, I got caned and hit a few times. Usually for talking. That was what I found hardest to stop. I never really did anything very bad. I was naughty, but probably not by today's standards.'

While Louise's memories of her teachers have faded with time, there was one she still remembers vividly

'There was one teacher, a Miss Jensen, that I liked very much. She was young, and very kind. She was the music teacher and she was quite talented. She was a concert singer and a concert pianist as well as being a teacher. I loved music of course, and she encouraged that in me. I played the flute in the school orchestra and was part of the choir. We had about 200 singers, it was actually very good.

'I remember listening to her sing. She had a nice voice, a mezzo-soprano if I remember correctly. I admired her, she was talented musically in a way that I probably wished I was.'

Louise has no distinct recollection of what became of Miss Jensen after Hitler's rise to power.

'I cannot remember if she was still teaching at the school when I graduated. I hope she survived the war. But who knows? If she did not, she would have been just one of so many.'

One thing that was certain is that, after 1932, those teachers interested in their own professional survival quickly abandoned old lesson plans in favour of instructions on Nazi policy and constant references to the Führer's greatness.

'Before 1933 I can remember that some of the teachers would get a little bit political about the current economic situation. There were occasionally comments about inflation, the French invading the Ruhr and about the humiliation of Versailles. But it was nothing over the top. Once Hitler became Chancellor however, there was a really rapid change. Versailles was now presented to us as a lunatic judgement, a crime against the German people. The loss of the First World War was blamed on traitors within the country. Everything was presented from Hitler's viewpoint. The message was loud and clear that he was saving the country.'

Louise's reaction, like that of all her classmates, was simply mute acceptance of the new order.

'We were children, too young to make judgements on such complex issues. As a child you are impressionable, you don't question much and you believe most of what you are told. I just absorbed everything I was taught and didn't give it all that much thought. Our class sizes were very large — about 50 in each class on average. With that many children, it is easy to not stand out, to just blend in with everyone else. I sat and listened, remembered what I needed to for exams and homework, and just ignored anything that I didn't think was useful. I was more concerned with singing in the choir, or playing sports. Hitler I couldn't really care less about ...'

The Jesuit dictum: 'Give me the child until he is seven and I will show you the man' was one Hitler embraced with almost frantic enthusiasm. Following his appointment as Chancellor, sweeping curriculum changes were introduced, along with a program of teacher training that ensured National Socialist doctrine was an inescapable facet of classroom life. By 1937, 97 per cent of all teachers belonged to the National Socialist

Teachers' Union. Every potential member had to submit an ancestry table in triplicate with official documents of proof before being accepted.[2] Those unwilling or unable to meet the rigid membership requirements had little choice but to find another profession.

'We had some teachers who just didn't turn up to school one day. At the time, I wondered why they left, but of course now I suspect they were either forced to leave or they simply refused to teach what Hitler had requested.'

A great deal of archival school material from before the Second World War has survived to the present day. Little of it makes subtle reading. Crude and heavy-handed in tone, the school books innocently read by Louise and her classmates are classic examples of the Nazi propaganda technique. Drawing on everyday events and examples, the texts attempt to combine valid educational objectives with socio-political dogma.

One of the most widely available books was the *Deutscher National-Katechismus*, or German National Catechism. A kind of guidebook to Nazi values, this emotive little tome was first published in 1934 and stridently upheld all the main tenets of Nazi philosophy — imperialism, racial purity and, perhaps most importantly, the need to subjugate individuality to the greater good of German nationalism.

> ... you belong to the German people just as every part of your
> body belongs to you. You are a link in a great chain, a part of the
> whole. Alone you are nothing, but when you live in your people
> you are everything.[3]

An undated question from a primary school mathematics exam is even more blatantly manipulative. Designed to familiarise the younger generation with the long-term government goal of euthanasing the mentally ill along with physically and intellectually disabled citizens, the question reads:

To keep a mentally ill person costs approximately four marks a day. There are 300,000 mentally ill people in care. How much do these people cost to keep in total? How many marriage loans of 1000 marks could be granted with this money?[4]

Other aspects of the Nazi curriculum more subtly disguised their real intent. Physical education, previously not a major part of German school life, soon occupied at least 15 per cent of the weekly class timetable. Ostensibly an extension of the fascist 'healthy mind, healthy body' principle and a means of keeping the master race in shape, the sports and athletic emphasis also ensured a ready supply of healthy young bodies for the war already being planned. Similarly, a decision in 1937 to allow students to choose whether or not to attend religious education class had a dual motivation. National Socialism claimed to be conservatively secular in its approach to Christianity. In truth this was simply a way of remaining onside with the majority of Germans who considered themselves both Christian and conservative — particularly in largely protestant Prussia where old values were deeply engrained. In fact Hitler and his top-ranking ministers had no time for any religion outside National Socialism. The Nazi Party was their church, and Adolf Hitler their god. Any other organised belief system outside their own was at worst a potential threat to their power and at best a slight on the greatness of the Führer.

Heinrich Himmler, head of the Schutzstaffel (SS) and the man most closely associated with the horrors of the concentration camps, was one prominent Nazi who believed Christianity to be simply inferior to the raw aggression and brash confidence of National Socialism. And, therefore, worthy of eradication.

How different is yonder pale figure on the cross, whose passivity and emphasised mien of suffering express only humility and self-abnegation, qualities which we, conscious of our heroic blood,

utterly deny ... the corruption of our blood caused by the
intrusion of this alien philosophy must be ended ...[5]

Himmler's frequent habit of speaking quietly to the portrait of Hitler
hanging in his office leaves little doubt as to where — or rather to
whom — his own faith was directed.[6]

The issue of anti-Semitism in Nazi education remains a complex
and, indeed, controversial one.

In an essay entitled 'Propaganda and Children during the Hitler
Years,' academic Mary Mills states that 'anti-Semitism was the
overwhelming topic in every school curriculum'. Lessons in racial
hatred began, she claims, as early as six years old and continued
through until graduation.[7]

The campaign to ensure most teachers were trained to follow the
official government line would seem to support the claim that German
children memorised racial hatreds along with their times tables and
proper nouns. There is also ample archival school material that displays
an undeniable and often disturbing level of anti-Semitism.

The same *Deutscher National-Katechismus* that encouraged the
subjugation of free will also contained various passages of overt anti-
Jewish sentiment. The Jews are described as the 'race which the
National Socialist race must fight against' and the children are warned
that the 'goal of the Jew is to make himself the ruler of humanity.
Wherever he comes he destroys works of culture. He is not a creative
spirit, rather a destructive spirit.'[8]

Many texts make reference to the alleged greed of Jews and their
apparent habit of betraying the national interest in return for money.
Avarice was the most frequently quoted Jewish 'crime' and despite a long
tradition of anti-Semitism amongst some sectors of German society, it was
a concept that only gained widespread currency after the 1918 defeat.

Trust No Fox on His Green Heath and No Jew On His Oath is perhaps
the best known surviving anti-Semitic children's book. First published

in 1936 and written by a young German woman called Elwira Bauer, it was not an official school text but rather a very popular picture book of rhyming fables.

A story titled 'The Cattle Jew' is a typical example.

There was once a Jew called Kohn
With 100,000 talers all his own
From cutting offers to the bone.
Greed of gold had sullied his soul.
Came a farmer in greatest need,
Cows and pigs he offered the Jew
For 120 Gulden new,
To free himself from binding debt.
The Jew, however, was not ashamed
To pay him half the price he named.
Away went cattle with grinning Jew.
The farmer was heartbroken too.
Misfortune dogs him more and more,
In Jewish hands there's death in store.[9]

In marked contrast, however, Louise cannot recall any overtly anti-Jewish slant to her classroom lessons.

'I can't remember ever being told by a teacher that we should hate the Jews. Nobody I knew in Wismar ever spoke like that. There would have been no reason for it. We had nothing against the Jews; they had done nothing to us. I have no memory of reading books at school that preached hatred to the Jews or anyone else. It was a long time ago but I seem to remember my books were just the usual sort that children read — stories about children having adventures and games and so on.'

As Louise remembers it, the Nazi influence on school life was concerned almost completely with the deification of Adolf Hitler.

'We were told constantly that everything good about Germany was as a result of Hitler. We were told to be grateful for what he had done for us and that we needed to obey him. He was like a demi-god really; that was the way he was presented to us.'

The discrepancy between the historical evidence and Louise's memory is perhaps best explained by the nature of Wismar itself and the fact that levels of Jewish persecution varied greatly between regions. Cities like Berlin and Munich appear to have been the epicentres of discrimination, although regional centres such as Worms, Brunswick and Kassel also rapidly developed a hard-line reputation. The East Prussian town of Neidenburg decided to deal with the 'Jewish issue' by expelling their entire Jewish population in 1936. Wismar though, having being an open port for centuries, was perhaps less intolerant of cultural differences than other parts of the country. While I could find no official figures on the size of the town's Jewish population before the Second World War, Louise remembers Jews as being quite a small minority.

'We had only a few Jewish children at my school. There was a Jewish girl in my class when I was quite young. I remember because she was not allowed to do religious education with us and had to sit on her own during those times.'

By the winter of 1938, that same girl would have been forbidden from attending school at all, courtesy of the draconian Nuremberg Laws.

'I can honestly say that during the early years of Hitler's dictatorship, I cannot remember ever being told outright by a teacher or another adult that Jews were bad. I suppose those messages could have been put to us subtly but, if they were, they certainly didn't make much of an impression on me. As a young girl, I never gave Jews a second thought really. I knew a few and that was it. They were just people like any other to me. Schools may have been different in other towns. I imagine it would have depended quite a bit on the individual teachers at each school. Perhaps those where the teachers were big supporters of the Nazi Party were more open and aggressive in what they taught.

'For me, I had no reason to be worried at that time about the Jews or what Hitler might be planning at first. There was no indication of the sort of person he was going to become. To me, it seemed that things were getting better in Germany, not worse. We were happy at school, even though the teachers beat us if we were naughty. Life was quite normal for the first few years; in fact, I would say people were happier than they had been since the War. Food was more plentiful, people had jobs again, and the economy was very good. Nobody was complaining. If my parents were suspicious or concerned about the direction in which the Nazis were taking Germany, they never mentioned it to me. But I suppose that they would have been well aware that this was not going to be a normal political party of the kind Germany had seen before.'

Indeed, the Fox family was not sheltered from the more dictatorial extremes of Nazism for very long.

In 1934 Louise's transition from primary to secondary school came with a new condition. Her father Fritz was forced to join the Nazi Party before her enrolment would be accepted.

'There was pressure on everyone to join the Party. If you wanted your children to go to a certain school, if you wanted to have a chance to get a promotion at work, if you didn't want other people to start wondering about how loyal you were to Germany. In the early days of Hitler at least, I think the message to join was fairly subtle but everyone knew that it was what you had to do. And at that time most people thought Hitler was doing a good job, so joining the Party wasn't necessarily seen as a bad thing.'

If apolitical Fritz had any reservations about his forced allegiance, he kept them to himself.

'I don't think my father was all that concerned about having to join. He just accepted it as something that had to be done. He was never an active member, he worked with the orchestra most nights and I don't think he ever attended many meetings. He did wear a badge on his lapel though — a little swastika.'

Others in Wismar were also experiencing pressure of a rather more sinister kind. The town's small Jewish population was beginning to become concerned at the government's increasingly strident anti-Semitism and, as troubling reports from Munich and Berlin reached the north, those Jews that could leave the country, did so. Others were not so fortunate.

Louise recalls her grandparents bemoaning the loss of their local doctor — a Jew who had treated them for many years and for whom they had great respect.

'He was a very kind man, my grandparents said. When people had no money to pay for a house call, he would come anyway. He was well liked by all his patients — German and Jew. He was in his eighties — not a young man at all. One day the SS came and took him away. We never found out what happened to him.'

It's not hard to make an informed guess though. Following the vast numbers of arrests of political opponents made after the Reichstag Fire in February 1933, Hermann Goering, then Germany's second most powerful Nazi and soon to play a pivotal role in Louise's life, decided to open special gaols to house the overflow of detainees. The name used for these new prisons was Konzentrationslager, or concentration camp.

Although the systemic policy of Jewish internment was not yet in place, there is little doubt that these camps, run by the SA in their usual brutal fashion, were the forerunners of Auschwitz. An estimated 700 prisoners died at these nascent Konzentrationslager in less than 12 months. Goering finally ordered them closed when he discovered that the SA were so happy in their new role that they were opening more camps without his permission.[10]

Over the next few years, life in Wismar took on a new, darker hue. The intoxicating optimism which had greeted the Führer's ascension to power in 1933 had begun to wane. While employment rates and general living conditions were much improved, the full impact of the

Nazi agenda was beginning to be felt, creeping like a stain across the fabric of ordinary life.

'People began to disappear,' Louise said simply. 'First it was some Jewish children in my school. One day they were there, the next they were gone. I didn't ask why, I suppose I just thought they'd moved away suddenly. I was still a child and I wouldn't really understand what was going on in Germany until the war a few years later.

'Then, a family on our street went. We didn't know what happened to them or why they disappeared. I don't think they were Jewish. People started not to talk about certain things, there were stories about people getting visits in the middle of the night and being arrested. I never knew anyone personally that this happened to, but everyone just had this sense that suddenly you had to be careful what you said.'

From mid-1933 onwards, all across Germany towns like Wismar saw their institutions, clubs and social committees hijacked and appropriated to the Nazi cause. None of the minutiae of life was spared, no matter how seemingly bland or innocuous. Town councils were purged of any unsympathetic elected officials; social democrats, former communists and ethnic minorities were forbidden to work in local industries and private businesses. Professional associations such as Doctors' Societies, workers' unions, hunting clubs (always an integral part of regional German life), even gardening and social clubs, came under Nazi control. In some instances, the Party simply insisted on a trusted Nazi being appointed chairman or president of the group. In other cases, all non-Party members were ostracised and more obedient souls put in their place.

In *The Coming of the Third Reich,* Richard J. Evans sums up the impact of Nazi indoctrination:

What social life remained was at the local inn, or took place in the privacy of people's homes. Individuals had become isolated except when they gathered in one Nazi organization or another.

Society had been reduced to an anonymous and undifferentiated mass and then reconstituted in a new form in which everything was done in the name of Nazism.

Like everything in life, however, even the steamroller tactics of the National Socialists had imperfections.

The process of co-ordination was less than perfectly carried out, and a formal adherence to the new order through, for example, attaching the name 'National Socialist' to a club, a society ... by no means implied a genuine ideological commitment on the part of those involved.[11]

The Nuremberg Laws, introduced in the autumn of 1935, spelt out the regime's racial agenda in uncompromising fashion. Only ethnically pure Germans were allowed the full benefits of citizenship. Jews were demoted to the status of residents with no voting privileges. Marriage and sexual relations between Jew and non-Jew were expressly forbidden.

While Louise has no clear memory of the introduction of the Nuremburg legislation, she admits that adult Germans 'must have known' how discriminatory they were and what the likely impact would be on the Jewish population.

'But that is dictatorship, you see,' she said. 'It makes cowards of us all.'

Those few willing to raise their voices to challenge the regime were largely drowned out by the relentless wave of Nazi propaganda.

By the time the Nuremberg Laws were set down, obtaining independent information about any aspect of German political, economic or social life was virtually impossible. Joseph Goebbels took his title as Reich Minister for Popular Enlightenment and Propaganda very seriously indeed.

Newspapers, magazines and even light entertainment such as movies and newsreels became nothing more than instruments of propaganda. Journalists with alleged Marxist or Jewish leanings were banned, opposition publications were closed and their staff often imprisoned. Films had to undergo a compulsory script censorship process before being allowed a release and those few independent moviemakers who passed Goebbels' strict criteria had to compete with the plethora of movies funded solely by the Party itself. Between 1933 and 1945, over 1000 Nazi-produced feature films were screened.[12]

Books deemed contrary to the public interest were banned — and, famously, burnt at stage-managed street rallies — while liberal academics, musicians, scientists and artists were placed under great pressure to either support the regime or get out of the way. Many, including Albert Einstein, the playwright Bertolt Brecht, composer Arnold Schoenberg and theatre director Max Reinhardt opted for the latter, while those who stayed found themselves under constant scrutiny, their works often publicly derided and their reputations smeared at every opportunity.

By 1937, such was the scope of Nazi control that Goebbels — deciding that modern art was overtly radical and taking his cue as always from Hitler who disliked modernity of any kind — had more than 16,000 paintings by artists such as Cézanne, Picasso, Munch and Van Gogh seized from the National Gallery in Berlin.

A display of work deemed suitable was then put in its place, while the confiscated works were exhibited in a small Berlin gallery under the title of 'Exhibition of Degenerate Art'. While the aim was to ridicule the modern paintings, the Goebbels plan backfired badly. More than two million Germans visited the 'degenerate' exhibition — far more than turned out to see the sanctioned display. A furious Goebbels closed the exhibition earlier than scheduled and sold most of the paintings overseas.[13]

Radio was the communication backbone of pre-war Germany. Even those without the resources or access to movies, books and galleries generally had a radio in their homes. It was inevitable that radio would be the prime vehicle for propaganda.

Gaining control of the many independent radio stations that existed pre-1933 was simple enough — Goebbels simply transformed them into branches of a Reich-controlled radio network, casting aside dissenters and those deemed not sufficiently loyal to the Party line. To ensure no one missed out on the message, Goebbels also began distributing cheap radios to every German household. Interestingly, these radios had a deliberately limited range to ensure that no foreign broadcasts could be picked up.

And it was an incident involving a radio that finally forced Louise to confront the truth about what her country and its people had become at Hitler's hands.

In one of the Fox household's rare moments of serendipity, Fritz, Lucy, Louise and little Gerda would gather together around the radio most days to listen to the classical music broadcast on Danish radio.

A love of good music was the one thread that bound husband and wife, parents and children together and Louise recalls how she always looked forward to the moment when the music would start, listening with delight as an unseen orchestra sent its exquisite melodies across the Baltic.

'The German stations had no good music at all. It was all marching bands and long speeches. So we listened to Danish radio instead. It was easy to pick up Danish stations from Wismar.

'One day though, someone came to our door and talked to my parents. They came back inside and told me that we couldn't listen to the Danish station any more. It was simply too dangerous. If we were caught we could all face the death penalty. I believe it was a neighbour who heard our music play and decided to warn us before my parents were discovered by someone more sympathetic to the Nazis.

'We were lucky really. By then, neighbours had already begun to turn on each other, sometimes even family members were encouraged to report their relatives if they thought they were up to anything suspicious.

'There was nothing political about that Danish station. It just played music, that's all. And yet we were not allowed to listen to it, we were not allowed to enjoy something that was doing no harm to anyone. From then on I realised just how much we were controlled. And how it was already too late to do anything about it.'

Another facet of Louise's life over which she had no influence was her education. The German school system at the time clearly differentiated between those students who wished to pursue university studies and those whose ambitions were a little less lofty.

Her mother had enrolled Louise to attend a school that finished at what was commonly known as intermediate level. Having not studied the core subjects compulsory for admittance to university, intermediate level students were ineligible for tertiary enrolment and were instead essentially groomed for life on the factory floor or in the secretarial pool. In contrast, Gerda would be allowed to attend university, later graduating with a degree in metallurgy.

Despite excellent academic results in primary school, Louise was never consulted about her educational path.

'It simply wasn't up to me,' she said, recalling a passivity and level of obedience amongst the youth of that time that modern adolescents would have great trouble comprehending. 'My parents made those choices for both me and my sister — there was no discussion. The schools that allowed you to go onto university were also much more expensive and my parents always had to watch money a little bit.'

The question as to whether she resented not being allowed a choice is met with a patient shrug.

'I had no say, no other choice. What else can you do but make the best of it?'

1937 was a nervous year. The Italians joined the German and Japanese military alliance, the French reinforced the Maginot Line along the border with Germany, 17,000 were killed by the Luftwaffe on a sunny day in the Spanish town of Guernica, Hitler signed a non-aggression pact with an anxious Poland and later that same day let his top officers in on a little secret — the only way for Germany to achieve its divine right to Lebensraum or living space would be at the expense of surrounding nations.

It was also the year when, aged 17, Louise Fox graduated from school and went off to work for the first time.

The rebellious, single-minded child had become a rebellious, single-minded young adult, albeit one still unable to escape her mother's dominion.

Dark-haired, black-eyed and quite distinctly un-Aryan in appearance, Louise had grown into a striking looking woman with a passion for fashion.

'I suppose I wasn't a tomboy any more. I still loved sport, I still really enjoyed running and being outdoors, but I also enjoyed being a girl too. I found that I loved clothes and fashion. Really girly things. People always said I had very good taste and I loved to dress up as much as I could, although I usually didn't have much money to spend. Hair, make-up, shoes; I loved to look nice,' she said.

Her new job however, was distinctly unglamorous. At her mother's insistence, Louise had accepted a three-year apprenticeship with a small manufacturing company in Wismar. The hours were long, the wages poor and the work stupefyingly dull.

'The company made hand basins and central heating, nothing very exciting. I mostly did book-keeping, writing out the bills, typing and so on. Basically, whatever office work needed to be done. I learnt on the job. It wasn't difficult work but I didn't enjoy it at all. It was very boring. I worked six days a weeks. My wages were very low as well. My contract said I was paid 15 marks per months in the first year, 25 in the second and 35 in the third and final year.'

For most young people, the most immediate reward of joining the workforce is the greater independence it brings. But for Louise, her new role in life brought no change to her status at home.

'My mother didn't treat me any differently just because I had a job. She still couldn't produce a single kind word for me — ever. And of course my parents continued to argue about anything and everything. My sister and I were by this time so used to their bickering that we just ignored it most of the time.'

While Gerda continued to enjoy her mother's favouritism, Louise found that a six-day working week still offered no respite from her mother's demands.

'There was always Sunday,' she explained wryly. 'I would spend hours every Sunday cleaning the apartment. "Get down on your knees and clean the corners!" she would shout at me. I'll never forget it. There I was, almost a grown woman and nothing had changed in all those years. I was still scrubbing corners for that woman.'

Her mother also appropriated the bulk of Louise's meagre wages in return for room and board. 'I had enough money to go to the hairdresser's once a month, or to buy a dress and maybe the movies occasionally. That was it.'

Developing a social life in the acrimonious atmosphere of the family home also proved impossible without resorting to subterfuge.

'My mother basically forbade me to go out with my friends. Although I was a late bloomer in terms of boys and the like, of course I was interested in them. But my mother was very strict. I wasn't allowed to even go to the movies with a group of friends, let along have a boyfriend. She was not quite as strict with female friends, provided she thought she knew what we were doing. My best friend was Elsa, a girl I had gone to school with. We spent a lot of time together and had great fun. She stayed in

Wismar during the war, and after I left Germany, I tried to stay in touch with her. But Wismar had become Communist by then and my letters were all intercepted. I had no way of contacting her and never heard from her again. I don't even know if she is still alive.'

Her mother's constant scrutiny left Louise with little option but to lie to her parents on a regular basis.

'I was a typical teenager I suppose and rebellious. I didn't like to be told what to do; I hated to be ordered around. And so I lied. It wasn't something that I wanted to do, but she gave me no choice. I started to sneak out and keep secrets from her. I would go out with a group of people, and tell her I was going to a girl's house to do knitting together — something like that. When I had a boyfriend, I kept it to myself. She never found out, thank God.'

Then, Louise felt nothing but bitter resentment for her mother's interference. More than 60 years later however, her rancour has been softened by a degree of understanding.

'I think she was frightened that I would share the same fate as her — falling pregnant and being forced to marry someone who wasn't right for you. She was a desperately unhappy woman and she transferred that unhappiness onto me. She blamed me for her predicament. But at the same time I think she was also trying to protect me in her own way.'

While the international community had been casting an increasingly fretful eye on Germany's military buildup and the more obvious excesses of Hitler's expansionist policy, the regime's legislated racial bigotry had raised fewer concerns.

True, there had been several public demonstrations in both London and Paris against Nazi oppression since 1933, but most members of the general public were neither aware of nor indeed overly concerned about the full extent of Germany's racial platform.

In pre-war Europe, anti-Semitism was far from a purely German affliction.

Cartoons portraying Jews as caricature Shylocks were common in British, French and US publications, with some overtly offensive pieces appearing as late as the mid-1930s.

The sarcastic use of the term 'the chosen people' was commonly employed throughout Britain to suggest that Jews regarded themselves as somehow superior to Christians.

The public attitude towards Jews was perhaps most famously captured by George Orwell in his classic essay 'Anti-Semitism in Britain'. Published during the Second World War, Orwell's essay argued that anti-Jewish feeling was quite widespread across all social classes in Britain and while, given 'the invariably gentle and law-abiding' nature of the English there was no chance they would follow Germany's brutal example, English anti-Semitism had not waned even as knowledge of Nazi atrocities became known.

He cites a middle-class London woman who offered the following assessment of Britain's Jewish community:

> Well, no one could call me anti-Semitic, but I do think the ways these Jews behave is too absolutely stinking. The way they push their way to the head of the queue and so on. They're so abominably selfish. I think they're responsible for a lot of what happens to them.[14]

On 7 November 1938, Herschel Grynszpan, a 17-year-old Polish Jew exiled in France, walked into the German Embassy in Paris armed with a pistol and a burning sense of outrage at his family's treatment by the Nazis. He fired five shots into Ernst vom Rath, a minor party official and embassy staffer. Berlin's reaction to Rath's death two days later was an unequivocal call for revenge.

In the pre-dawn darkness of 10 November 1938, a calculated wave of violence against Jews was unleashed at the behest of Joseph Goebbels.

In a few shocking hours at least 236 Jews were murdered, including 43 women and 13 children in Berlin alone. More than 600 were permanently maimed.[15]

Synagogues were burnt to the ground, Jewish homes and businesses looted in co-ordinated attacks throughout the country. Some 30,000 Jews were taken from their homes and sent to concentration camps. Many of those would never be seen alive again.

To the Nazis, the attack was a show of strength, an exercise in muscle flexing that also offered the chance to get their hands on valuable Jewish goods and property.

British journalist Hugh Carleton Greene, reporting in the London *Daily Telegraph,* glimpsed something entirely more bestial:

Mob law ruled Berlin ... and hordes of hooligans indulged in an orgy of destruction. I have seen several anti-Jewish outbreaks in Germany during the last five years, but never anything as nauseating as this.

Racial hatred and hysteria seemed to have taken complete hold of otherwise decent people. I saw fashionably dressed women clapping their hands and screaming with glee, while respectable middle-class mothers held up their babies to see the 'fun'.[16]

For the first time, the plight of Germany's Jews made front page headlines around the world. Shocked and scandalised editorials issued forth from London, Paris and New York. Goebbels, who had hoped that the pogrom would elevate him in Hitler's favour, unexpectedly found himself under intense criticism, both from Hitler himself who was concerned about possible damage to key international relationships and Goering who — incredibly — was worried about the cost of replacing all the shattered shop windows.

The outrage of the world's press did not unfortunately extend to their governments. While most leaders made formal speeches condemning the actions, they declined to sanction the Germans in any significant way. Franklin Roosevelt recalled the US ambassador from Germany but later sent him back to Berlin. A few months later, Roosevelt would decline to offer refugee status to 20,000 German Jewish children.

Sensing the inherent lack of will behind all the international protestations, Hermann Goering issued a typically arrogant press statement.

'No Jew had a hair on his head touched,' he said. 'Thanks to the outstanding discipline of the German people, only a few windows were broken in the riots.'[17]

It was his reference to those few broken windows that inspired a bemused Nazi rank and file to christen the event Kristallnacht, or the Night of Broken Glass.

Goering ultimately solved the matter of paying for the huge repair bill by fining the Jewish community one billion marks for damages.

The tepid response by world leaders would later draw this remark from a German newspaper:

'We can see that one likes to pity the Jews ... but no state is prepared to accept a few thousand Jews. This ... serves to justify Germany's policy against Jewry.'[18]

The ferocity of Kristallnacht even extended to Wismar. Louise recalls walking past shattered shop fronts and picking her way through debris-strewn cobblestones, amazed at the destruction and ignorant of the true motivation behind it.

'I thought there had been a riot of some kind. There was broken glass on the streets and some of the shops had been broken into. They had shattered the windows with brick and bits of rubble. It was nothing like what happened in the bigger cities though. Wismar was a much smaller place and a bit isolated from what went on in Berlin or

Munich. There wasn't even a synagogue in Wismar — in many other places the synagogues had been burnt down. But I could see that some of the shops that were destroyed were Jewish owned. One belonged to the family of a girl I had been to school with. The family had disappeared a few weeks beforehand — I found out later they had actually escaped and ended up in Vladivostok. So they were lucky. Their shop was ruined — who knows what would have happened to them if they had stayed in Wismar much longer?

'What we didn't realise was that the destruction of the shops had been carried out all over Germany on the same night — that it was all planned. We thought it was just something that had happened in our town. There was nothing about it in the local papers and people were reluctant to discuss it too much amongst themselves. We knew that something terrible was happening to Germany; we knew we had lost our freedoms. And we'd realised that the Jews were being arrested and discriminated against. But I still didn't know the full extent of what Hitler was planning to do. Nobody did. And it was very dangerous to ask too many questions.'

Louise was feeling stifled both by the monotony of her work and her mother's own brand of oppression when a partial solution presented itself. Concerned at the waning attendance at Hitler Youth meetings and rallies, the government announced that membership had become compulsory. Louise dutifully joined the Bund Deutscher Mädel, or German Girls' League, the female branch of the Hitler Youth.

Organised youth movements had been an accepted part of German life — at least for boys — since the late 1800s. But it was Hitler who realised their untapped potential as a means of firmly instilling Nazi beliefs in the young, and as a reservoir for soldiers in a future war.

National Socialist youth clubs first made an appearance in 1926. They initially struggled to compete with the myriad sporting, nature and religious boys' organisations already in existence. As the party grew in popularity, membership of the Hitler Youth (a name suggested by Rudolf Hess) skyrocketed. In 1932, more than 100,000 boys were enrolled.

With its militaristic format and emphasis on physical fitness, obedience and adoration of the Führer, the aims of Hitler Youth were clear. In fact, Hitler himself had spelt them out clearly years before in *Mein Kampf*: '... a less-educated, but physically healthy individual with a sound, firm character, full of determination and will power, is more valuable to the Voelkisch community than an intellectual weakling ...'[19]

Amidst the running races and Sieg Heils, the chillingly fatalistic aspects of Hitler's philosophy were never far away. At ten years of age, new recruits were presented with a dagger inscribed 'Blood and Honour' while some branches held regular mock funerals as a way of psychologically preparing boys for death in battle. 'We are born to die for Germany' was a favourite slogan.

The mood was somewhat less intense at both The German Girls' League and Jungmädelgruppe, its junior division. Established in 1930, Bund Deutscher Mädel's aim was not to create soldiers but passive bearers of healthy Aryan children to populate the Thousand-year Reich of Hitler's fantasies.

Like the boys' divisions, the emphasis was primarily on physical education. Before it became compulsory, girls wanting to join had to be able to run 60 metres in 14 seconds, throw a ball 12 metres, complete a two-hour march and swim 100 metres.[20]

Duty, sacrifice, discipline and physical self-control were the key tenets of the girls' education. Girls were also fed a steady diet of National Socialist dogma, although not in the copious quantities of their male counterparts.

Girls were reminded to avoid all contact with Jews and other racially inferior people and informed that motherhood was the highest office a good German woman should wish to aspire to. Husbands were to be obeyed, houses cleaned and children raised according to Nazi guidelines.

The German Girls' League's ideal woman was an oddly old-fashioned creature modelled on early 19th century notions of female purity. A demure dress sense was enforced and girls were encouraged to wear their hair in traditional plaits or braided into so-called 'Gretchen wreaths'. Short, coloured or permed hair was frowned upon, and occasionally League members who dared to adopt an unorthodox hairstyle had their heads shaved as punishment.

For Louise, the Girls' League was nothing more than harmless fun.

'It was a chance to get away from my mother and meet up with my friends. Even she couldn't stop my going to the meetings once a week; she could do nothing about it. I really loved going.'

Although Girls' League meetings were off-limits to men, Louise found plenty of other diversions on offer. Always a keen sportswoman, she relished the hikes and sporting competitions on offer during the warmer months.

She was far less enthusiastic about lessons in Nazi history and doctrine but, having spent most of her childhood absorbing propaganda, believed it was a small price to pay for the social opportunities and relative freedoms on offer within the organisation.

'We spent a fair bit of time listening to one so-called teacher or another giving us the latest propaganda. We had to learn Nazi songs off by heart, which I found boring. We were told about Hitler's ideas for Germany, which of course were a load of rubbish but we didn't know any better. Some girls might have taken them all very seriously, but the ones I knew didn't. We just listened because we had to and then forgot about it.

'You must realise that people my age at the time had been brought up with Hitler in power. We were used to doing what we were told and being obedient. But that doesn't mean we all believed in what we were hearing or that we cared about it.

'I do remember that I would get annoyed sometimes about how often we were told to thank Hitler for things. If we went hiking and the weather was warm, we should thank Hitler. If we were taken on an outing somewhere, we should thank Hitler. Everything was his doing. It was as if no one else existed in the world. I used to find that very silly, even back then.'

The League's encouragement of early marriage and motherhood was another tenet that Louise refused to take seriously.

'They were always talking about how we needed to get married and have children for Germany. How we needed lots of pure Germans to protect the country from our enemies. I didn't believe that. My friends and I were still too young to think about marriage, so we didn't think it applied to us. I had so little freedom as it was, there was no way I wanted to settle down.'

While chastity before marriage was constantly held up as an ideal virtue, there is plenty of evidence that the Nazi definition of morality was pragmatic to say the least.

Richard Grunberger relates the story of how 100,000 members of the Hitler Youth and German Girls' League travelled to Berlin to attend the Nuremberg Rally. At least 18 teenage girls returned home pregnant.[21]

Heinrich Himmler made quite an impact when he addressed a large gathering of German Girls' League officials and members. Jutta Rudiger, head of the organisation at the time, recalled:

He said that if there was a war a lot of men would be killed and therefore the nation needed more children, and it wouldn't seem such a bad idea if a man, in addition to his wife, had a girlfriend who would also bear his children. And I must say all my leaders were sitting there with their hair standing on end.[22]

In truth, protecting the honour of German maidens should have been amongst the least of Frau Rudiger's concerns.

Hitler's policy of Lebensraum had long been a vote winner for the party. While his complete views on race and eugenics were not particularly well known outside interested political circles (or those who had managed to wade through *Mein Kampf)* prior to his Chancellorship, his support of German expansionism had been a key component of his election platform.

His promise of not only reuniting all German-speaking people under one banner but also to push German borders into Russian-occupied areas, providing both protection from the Jewish/Marxist menace emanating from the East and additional territory for a growing population, was widely applauded by an electorate still licking its war wounds.

Playing cleverly on the population's fervent nationalism, once in power the Nazis transformed the long-held and cherished dream of a greater German empire into official government policy.

It began with the remilitarisation of the Rhineland in 1936, something strictly forbidden by the terms of Versailles.

Emboldened by the international community's apathetic response to this show of German defiance, the Reich decided to pick up the pace. In 1938 Austria was annexed in a bloodless coup orchestrated from Berlin and given invaluable support from within by the Austrian Nazi Party. Hitler himself drove triumphantly down the main street of Linz, his Austrian home town, gleefully acknowledging the cheers of the stage-managed crowd.

The Sudetenland was next. Formerly part of Austria, this region had been lost to Czechoslovakia in 1919 as a condition of the Treaty of St Germain. Hitler demanded that the three million German-speaking residents of the Sudetenland — along with the area's significant resources of coal and steel manufacturing, be returned to the Fatherland. Desperate to avoid war at all costs, British Prime Minister Neville Chamberlain opted to sacrifice the Sudetenland to the cause of world peace, extracting promises that Germany would respect Czechoslovakia's now-redrawn borders.

Predictably, German tanks rolled into Prague on the morning of 15 March 1939. Czechoslovakia had officially ceased to exist.

It says much for the universal single-mindedness of adolescence that while Louise was aware of the gathering speed of German aggression — Austria, the Sudetenland, Czechoslovakia falling like dominos — her main focus and that of her friends resolutely remained 'boys and enjoying ourselves'.

'We didn't talk about things like that. We knew that Germany was expanding, but we were only told what the government wanted us to know. For example, Austria: that was never, ever described as an invasion; always as a positive thing. Austria and Germany had so much in common, so many ties that most people thought it was wonderful that they had joined us. We didn't know the truth of the matter and, to be honest, I wasn't really concerned with such things. I don't think teenagers today would react in the same way as we did. We were much more innocent I think and much more controlled by everyone — our parents, and the government.'

But while remilitarising the Rhineland and annexing Austria could easily be dismissed as simply taking back what was rightfully German to begin with, the Nazis were aware that their plans for Czechoslovakia and Poland would not be so widely applauded by the general public.

In order to repress any growing alarm and maintain public confidence in the regime, Goebbels resorted to his favourite form of defence — deception.

It began, as always, with radio and newspaper reports. Front pages and special news bulletins all began to carry stories about suppression of German minorities in Czechoslovakia. Often hysterical in tone and lurid in detail, these reports told of Germans being forced from their homes, of mass arrests — even of genocide.

Hans Fritzsche was the head of both the German Press Division and, later, of the Nazi radio network. He had direct editorial control over more than 2000 German daily newspapers and magazines, and every radio station in the country. Arrested and tried for war crimes at Nuremberg, his defence testimony shed valuable light on the thoroughness and totality of the Nazi propaganda machine.

> ... it was in February that I received the order from the Reich Press Chief ... to bring the attention of the press to the efforts for independence in Slovakia and the continued anti-German coalition politics of the Prague government. I did this.
>
> The daily paroles of the Reich Press Chief ... show the wording of the corresponding instructions. These were the typical headlines of leading newspapers of the German daily press at the time ... (1) the terrorising of Germans within the Czech territory by arrest, shooting of Germans by the State police, destruction of German homes by Czech gangsters, concentration of Czech forces on the Sudeten frontier; (2) the kidnapping, deporting and persecuting of Slovakian minorities by the Czechs; (3) the Czechs must get out of Slovakia; (4) secret meetings of Red functionaries in Prague.[23]

Louise remembers those media reports well.

'There were a lot of German people in Czechoslovakia and they had been trying to gain some independence for quite some time. Everyone knew that; it was the truth. So when the government started telling us these people were being attacked and killed, we believed it. It seemed quite possible. We heard horrible stories of German families, women and children, being murdered by the Czechs. Hitler and the others said that they had no choice but to go into Czechoslovakia to stop the killings and rescue the Germans. I never questioned that. Perhaps some of the older people were suspicious, but if they were, they would have kept it to themselves for fear of being arrested. I certainly never heard my parents express doubts about what was being reported on the radio. Younger people like me, we just accepted what we were told. Government lies were all we had ever known.

'And that is the most insidious thing about living in a dictatorship. Through fear and propaganda, the dictator encourages the people to stop thinking critically about things. And after a while, that is what happens. The older people may know the truth, but they are too frightened to say anything. The younger people, they just don't know any better.

'Today, in a democracy like Australia, there are so many different sources of information and people are free to disagree with the government whenever they choose. And yet, even here, I sometimes think people are easily misled by government or media lies. No wonder we were so easily led back in those days.'

At the 1938 Nuremberg rally, Hermann Goering gave official voice to Germany's intentions towards Czechoslovakia. Speaking to the thousands of assembled Party faithful, he said:

An insignificant segment of Europe is making life unbearable for mankind. The Czechs, that miserable pygmy race without any culture — nobody even knows where they came from — are oppressing a civilized race and behind them can be seen Moscow and the eternal face of the Jewish fiend.[24]

There would have been few in the crowd — or even throughout greater Germany — who would have doubted the essential truth of his words.

The invasion of Czechoslovakia — a wholly sovereign nation with nothing in common with Germany except proximity — proved to be a turning point. No longer able to excuse Hitler's aggression as merely a policy of German reunification, Chamberlain and his French counterpart Edouard Daladier were quick to publicly guarantee the border of Poland, the nation most obviously next in German sights. The victors of the First World War were finally drawing a line in the sand — albeit one that came far too late for the millions already suffering under imposed Nazi rule.

Hitler — against the advice of many of his leading generals and despite the fact that both the German army and air force remained significantly under-strength and under-prepared — decided to call their bluff.

At dawn on 1 September 1939, the German battleship *Schleswig-Holstein* opened fire on the Polish garrison at Danzig, now known as Gdansk. They were to be the first shots fired of the Second World War. At the same time, some 60 German divisions supported by 1300 aircraft entered Poland in a Blitzkrieg-style attack and headed towards Warsaw.

At noon on 3 September, Britain declared war on Germany. France followed suit five hours later.

Louise was at home with her family when the declaration of war came over the radio.

'I was completely shocked. I never expected war. We had been told that going into Czechoslovakia and Poland was justified, so it was a complete surprise to find that other countries were willing to start fighting us over the matter. Again, the people knew nothing of what was really going on in Germany and the rest of the world. We were duped by the government. It was so soon after the First World War. I couldn't believe that Germany had been stupid enough to do it all over again. I remember thinking, we lost the first war and suffered so much. Why on earth would the government put the people through it all again?'

The reaction of Fritz and Lucy was rather more muted.

'They didn't really say much about it. It was a little strange I suppose, but they never discussed it with us very much at all. I'm sure they talked about it to each other, but perhaps they didn't want to scare Gerda and I. Perhaps they were too worried that being concerned about war might get them into trouble. As for me, more than anything, I was very, very frightened.'

3 FIGHTING HITLER'S WAR

Unhappy is the land that is in need of heroes.
— *Bertolt Brecht*

EXPERIENCE IS AT ONCE the best and most ruthless of teachers.

In 1914, the German public had responded to the call to arms with gusto. Political parties on the left and right called off their constant bickering in a show of unprecedented solidarity. Kaiser Wilhelm declared that a Burgfrieden (national truce) had been called across all sectors of German political and social life, noting proudly (and one suspects with a great deal of relief) to the Reichstag that 'I do not know any parties any more'. Political graffiti were replaced with the cheekily optimistic declaration 'I'll see you in Paris', and almost everyone was convinced that the war would not only be short, but was inherently just.

Twenty-five years and millions of lost lives later, ordinary Germans were far more muted in their response to another round of international conflict.

'Our parents and grandparents had already lived through one war. They knew the consequences, they knew from bitter experience what war means to people's everyday lives. I imagine the first time around the war seemed like a necessary thing — perhaps even an adventure for some people. Germans were very patriotic then and it would have been easy to stir them up into thinking that a war was something we could win easily and that would even be good for the country. But, after the disaster of the First World War, nobody thought such nonsense anymore. The adults knew what we were in for and of course, they were really worried about what would happen this time.

'Naturally, there were no demonstrations in Wismar against the war; people didn't even talk to each other about it in public. But you could tell by people's faces that they were concerned and nervous. I'm sure my parents had a number of conversations about it — when they listened to news on the radio they often looked very concerned. But they didn't say much to Gerda and me. Children were mostly seen and not heard in those times, and I know they wouldn't have wanted to worry us anyway. But there was a definite sense of concern in Wismar, in my home, in the streets, in the shops and at school. Little was said aloud, but it was an uneasy time for many.'

Undoubtedly the most nervous of all were young men of draft age. Hitler had reintroduced military conscription on 16 March 1935, at the same time announcing the creation of a 36-division Wehrmacht (army). Both developments were in complete defiance of the terms of Versailles.

With typical bombast and in a move clearly designed to stir up German nationalism, he then declared the establishment of a Heroes' Memorial Day on 17 March to remember the fallen from the Great War. Hitler's speech was made amidst the ornate splendour of the Berlin State Opera House, and was followed by a sombre — and utterly appropriate — rendition of the funeral march from Beethoven's 'Eroica' Symphony.

'Not one of the boys my age I knew wanted to go and fight. They all waited until they were forced to go. In the First World War, the men had been more eager to fight. Now, they were being told by older people not to go until they had to. There may have been a few men who joined up when they didn't have to because of love of their country or because they were real Nazis. But there was no sense of enthusiasm about fighting. Those boys just did what they had to do. There was no choice in the matter.'

One of the first young men to be forced to fight Hitler's war was her long-time friend, Hanse.

'We used to play in the sandbox together. I had known him all my life. He was made to join the army — he didn't want to go. I don't recall ever discussing it with him in an open way — it was not the sort of thing that you really talked to anybody about unless they were family members or extremely close friends. By the time the war started, I did not see Hanse so frequently any more. But I heard from others that he was reluctant to go. He must have been very frightened. I did not say goodbye to him, something I regret now. He was killed by machine gun fire a few months after leaving Wismar.'

The declaration of war had an immediate impact on everyday life in the town.

Rationing was introduced within days of the Polish invasion, although it would remain more of an inconvenience than a serious deprivation for at least another year.

'The rations were actually quite generous, so I don't think anyone minded very much. At least for the first two years of the war there was still a good range of food to choose from and the amount each person was allowed was good. There weren't any food shortages at first, and no long queues at shops or anything like that. Nothing like it had been during the 1920s, when food shortages had been really desperate. We used a coupon system, the same as they did in Britain later on. You needed coupons even to go to dinner in a restaurant, and if you were careful with them, you would have enough for a nice meal and a glass or two of wine as well.

'From what I recall of that time, nobody went hungry; at least not at first. The food we ate was plain and basic — there were very few luxuries as we know them today — but there was enough for everyone to eat. Bread, grains, vegetables, a little fruit and a little meat

— we had enough. People still went out sometimes in the evening, although obviously not as frequently as they may have done before. In the early days of rationing, there was a sense in Wismar that life was still going on — perhaps not quite normally, but the war was not completely dominating every aspect of our lives. I think there was a sense of relief actually — that perhaps this time around things might not be as grim as they had been in the first war. People still had hope.'

In fact, the apparent generosity of the Nazi rationing system was built on false preferences. The Weimar era had taught Hitler that a hungry nation is more likely to challenge the status quo than a well-fed one. In an effort to feed both the civilian population and the armed forces, the Nazis had begun a deliberate programme of taking food and raw materials from occupied lands, even before the invasion of Poland. Like all that they imposed, the new policy was harsh, racially motivated and utterly inflexible.

'The German people come before all other peoples for food,' Goering declared during the war, alluding to a system which saw German nationals both at home and abroad receive the lion's share of food supplies, at the expense of other people living in occupied territories. In fact, a Nazi memo circa 1942 baldly states how food was to be distributed throughout the occupied territories. German nationals were to receive '100% of meat rations, Czechs 86%, French 51%, Serbs 36%, Slovenes 29%, Jews 0%.'[1]

In the Jewish quarter of Warsaw, mortality figures clearly reflect the outcome of the Nazi food policy. In July 1941, 1316 deaths from illness were recorded in the area. In August that number had climbed to 1729; by September, it was over 2000. Anaemia rates rose by 113 per cent amongst Poles and more than 435 per cent amongst Jews in that same year.[2]

For many non-Aryans the spectre of death by starvation was an even more pressing concern than what might await them in one of the Nazi concentration camps.

The source of their daily meals was not revealed to ordinary Germans until after the war was over.

'Yes, most people in Germany only found out after the war was over that others had been deliberately starved so that they might eat. At the time, the average person would have had no idea. Food was either in the shop or it was not. Why would anyone ask where it came from? Of course, after I became involved in the Luftwaffe, I quickly realised that the armed forces had access to food and goods that were clearly stolen from the enemy. But did I ever know for sure that the Jews were being starved in the ghetto, or that the Serbs were being used as slave labour and not being fed? No, I did not. This was war. People were only ever told what they needed to know. How could I know such details? And even had I known, what could I have done about it? Told Hitler to stop? War is bigger than any one person. Dictatorship is bigger than the individual who wishes to fight against it.'

What, I wondered, does she think her family and her neighbours might have done had they realised the terrible human cost involved in the rationing system?

It's a question Louise is able to answer with a surprising lack of hesitation.

'I don't think most people would have believed it. They would have thought it was fantasy — a ridiculous story. Yes, it is true that we already knew by then that Hitler was a very determined person. And we knew that some of our personal liberties had been taken away. Some people would also have known that dissenters, Jews, homosexuals and others were being put in prison camps. But to have believed that our own government was capable of cruelty on such a scale — I don't think many people would have accepted that without some sort of proof.

'The idea that Germans were somehow crueller or more hard-hearted than other people about such things — that comes from hindsight, from knowing about the atrocities that were carried out in our name. We didn't see ourselves like that at the time, and certainly most people I knew were good and decent. They weren't killers and torturers. If I were to tell you the Australian government was secretly enslaving and killing thousands of people in another country, would you believe me? I don't think so.

'And later on, when the rations grew short and people were really hungry, if they had discovered the truth at that point, they still would have eaten the food. They may have been sad, even angry, but they would also have known that it was a question of survival. Does starving yourself stop anyone else from being starved? When there is nothing left to do but try to stay alive, kindness and morality go out the window.'

At around the same time as rationing was introduced, the tone of Louise's German Girls' League meetings became more intense, with the emphasis shifting from sports to a continual justification of Germany's involvement in the war.

'We still sang Nazi songs and played outdoors, but now everything was related back to the war. We were told that Germany was the victim and that we were surrounded by enemies who wanted not just Hitler's downfall, but that of everyone in Germany. Our teachers constantly reminded us of our duty and how we must play our part in helping Germany win the war. In those early days there was never any question that we would win the war. They always talked about when we would have victory, not if.'

The weekly lectures at Bund Mädel were merely one small cog in the Nazi propaganda machine.

'The newspapers and radio — that was all we had to tell us what was going on with the war. And they all said the war was the fault of our enemies and that although we had no choice but to fight, we would be victorious. We were told the need for Lebensraum was one of the key reasons for the war — with a population of 60 million people Germany was overcrowded and would not progress properly until we had more space. Other countries in Europe wanted to deny us that space, to stop our progress. To doubt that the war was justified or that we were going to win — that would have been traitorous. The war was necessary, something that had to be done. That is what we were told and that was what I believed for quite some time. Dr Goebbels was always on the radio or in the newspapers, even more than Hitler I would say. I remember quite well listening to his speeches. He was very charismatic; he sounded very educated as well as very emotional when he spoke. Whatever he said sounded to me like it came from his heart; that it was the truth. He was an excellent communicator and he had a wonderful way with words. Looking back, I suppose it is obvious that there was hatred in his words, that a lot of what he was asking of us required someone else to suffer. But at the time, it didn't seem that way. It sounded like he wanted to protect Germany, that we were the ones under attack from others and were doing nothing more than defending ourselves.'

In an article which appeared in the Nazi weekly illustrated magazine, *Illustrierter Beobachter*, in late 1939, Goebbels laid the blame for hostilities firmly at the feet of the British, painting a picture of a crumbling society terrified at losing its dominance to an enlarged and reinvigorated German nation.

We did not want war. England inflicted it on us. English
plutocracy forced it on us. England is responsible for the war and
it will have to pay for it. We are acting consistently with
Nietzsche's words 'Give a shove to what is falling'.[3]

The other main thrust of early Nazi war propaganda was the suggestion that the conflict would be a brief one.

'All our newspaper and radio reports suggested that the war would be all over in six months. At first, I doubted that could be true — we all still had fresh memories of similar promises made during the First

World War. But then, when the months passed and no bombs were dropped and no foreign troops invaded, I started to hope that it was true.'

The Nazi emphasis on the brevity of the war arose both from a desire to placate a decidedly uneasy populace and a genuine belief amongst some of the Nazi hierarchy that victory was indeed a veritable *fait accompli*.

In correspondence with Italian government officials in late 1939 Hitler himself suggested that the war — which he referred to at the time as the English War and, later, as the Great German War of Liberation — would be over by 1940. In truth, the Allied inaction in the seven months since they opted to throw down the gauntlet to Hitler had given him every reason for such optimism. The so-called Phoney War (referred to by Germans at the time as the Sitzkrieg — an alternative to Blitzkrieg that involved lots of sitting around and doing nothing) was an odd period of calm before the approaching military storm. While Germany and Russia carved up Poland to their mutual benefit, Britain and France appeared unwilling or unable to retaliate. True, the British deployed some 158,000 men and 25,000 vehicles into France immediately after the invasion of Poland, but the force was woefully inadequate in comparison with the Nazi forces. The French had placed all their eggs in one basket, believing that a heavily enforced Maginot Line would prove impenetrable.

There is no reason to dismiss the possibility that Hitler honestly believed there was a chance for a quick victory. As early as 1937, Goering was telling a visiting British officer, Group Captain Christie — with whom he had struck up an unlikely friendship in 1933 — that he hoped Britain might turn a blind eye to the eventual German invasion of Russia.[4] Goering quite openly discussed a future continental Europe where Germany would hold sway with Italian support. France would lose its sovereignty, a fate not shared by Britain, provided she kept out of mainland affairs.

Goering referred to this future world as Mitteleuropa and suggested to Christie that it could be acquired gradually, without the need to launch a second international conflict.

If Britain, and later the USA, had acquiesced as hoped, Mitteleuropa could have become a reality and Hitler's predictions of a short, limited war may have proved accurate.

By September 1939, however, Goering's essential pragmatism had reasserted itself.

'Today's war is a total war, whose end no one can approximately foretell,' he wrote.[5]

It would be safe to say that a German-based Swiss carpenter by the name of George Elser was another with doubts about Hitler's ability to save Germany from another bloody and protracted conflict.

Outraged at Nazi suppression of human rights and convinced that the regime's aggressive foreign policy would ultimately destroy Germany, Elser devised a plan to assassinate Hitler after the invasion of the Sudetenland in 1938. He spent a month digging a secret tunnel into the Burgerbrau Beer Cellar in Munich, the venue for the annual reunion of veterans of the 1923 Beer Hall Putsch, knowing that Hitler always attended. A time bomb was planted behind a column and scheduled to explode during one of the Führer's notoriously long-winded speeches. For once, though, Hitler ran out of things to say. His speech ended earlier than scheduled and he left the building eight minutes before the bomb went off, leaving eight dead and 65 wounded in its wake.

Elser was captured attempting to cross the border into Switzerland and tortured into confessing. He spent the next six and a half years in concentration camps, before being shot by SS officers just fourteen days before Germany surrendered. Goebbels seized on the attack as evidence of British interference in German affairs, claiming that Elser was in fact a British operative. Research conducted after the war would prove he was in fact acting entirely alone and without any particular political allegiance. Elser would be the first of many to attempt to end the Supreme Commander's life.

Six years of Nazi rule had created a secretive, fearful society where personal opinions were closely guarded and criticism of the ruling regime was a clandestine and dangerous business. The war offered an excuse to further restrict personal freedoms and to pull the reins of oppression even tighter.

'We were always wary about talking out loud about controversial things — we realised the Gestapo had informants everywhere. You could trust nobody: not my teachers at school, not my neighbours, not my parents' friends even. If they confided in other adults or in my grandparents, I was not aware of the fact. They said little to us about current events really, although we were cautioned to be careful what we said. It wasn't something we needed to be continually reminded of, either; it was clear from the atmosphere in Wismar that talking out loud could get you into a lot of trouble.

'But when the war started, things just got worse. We knew the Gestapo would be looking for people they thought were traitors or not supporting the war. It meant that you could never trust anyone really, and that you learnt not to question or to complain very much — even when you were at home,' Louise said.

Just before 1939, Himmler had ordered police units in every German village, town and city to draw up lists of locals suspected of being Enemies of the State. Those on the list included not only the usual suspects such as Jews, socialists and homosexuals, but also those who attended church too often and failed to concentrate adequately on Nazi doctrine, those overheard criticising virtually any aspect of the regime, and even those overheard making a joke at Hitler's expense. The Gestapo were also granted the power to arrest anyone merely on the suspicion that they were about to do wrong.

Once arrested, detainees were given three minutes to pack a suitcase and were then escorted to the nearest police cell. Once inside they were ordered to sign a D-11 form, an order for protective custody. Those who declined to sign were beaten into submission. Once a request for protective custody had been filed, the prisoner was granted their wish — protection in one of the concentration camps.

'The most frightening thing about the Gestapo was that they were mostly nameless, faceless people. They didn't usually wear uniforms; they weren't necessarily military-type people at all. They were often just citizens who for whatever reason decided to join. It was their normality that gave them their power, really. The Gestapo could have been anyone in Wismar — the butcher, the teacher, the fellow living down the road. You never knew, so it was always best to treat everyone like they were a potential enemy. There was no doubt there were Gestapo in Wismar — there were too many stories of people being questioned and others just vanishing. So, we all lived life on a razor's edge.'

Such was the subjugation of Wismar's citizens that a large new factory built on the edge of town just before the invasion of Poland was noted but scarcely commented on.

'I did wonder what it was for, but we knew better than to ask questions like that. I'm sure some of the adults would have known — and plenty of people in the town had jobs in and around the site, so they would have realised what it was. I never really thought about it — there was so much going on at the time that I didn't really under-stand, and this new building just seemed like another unsolved mystery to me.'

In fact the building was secretly producing Dorniers flying boats for the German military. It — and Wismar by default — would later become the target of a heavy Allied bombing campaign.

Ten days after Germans troops marched into Prague, an official-looking letter arrived at the Fox apartment, addressed to nineteen-year-old Louise. Its message was uncompromising and to the point.

'It was an order from the local anti-aircraft commandant. I was to join the Air Force, the Luftwaffe. Immediately. I was told to go to work in the administration section of the anti-aircraft battalion in Wismar FLAK, Division 24.

'My apprenticeship was not finished, but that didn't matter. My employer gave me a certificate anyway and wished me luck It must have been a great inconvenience to him, but what could he do? Many businesses were in the same situation already. You couldn't argue with the government.'

Nor could you take issue with their insistence that everyone working with the armed forces in any capacity — even headstrong young girls whose love for pretty dresses, gossip and boys far outweighed any vague admiration they might have had for the Führer or his maniac vision — must take an Oath of Allegiance to the regime.

Louise still clearly remembers the day when she stood before the division commandant, wearing her best dress, hair and makeup perfect as always, right arm raised self-consciously in the air, index and middle finger extended skyward in the official oath position.

During the Hindenburg era all German soldiers had been obliged to take an oath, swearing loyalty to Germany and her people. After Hindenburg's death, Hitler had the traditional oath rewritten almost immediately to reflect his own ambitions.

I swear by God this sacred oath that I shall render unconditional
obedience to Adolf Hitler, the Führer of the German Reich,
supreme commander of the armed forces, and that I shall at all
times be prepared, as a brave soldier, to give my life for this oath.[6]

There is no reference to loyalty towards Germany itself, or to its people. Louise, and the many millions of her countrymen who were also obliged to take the oath, were announcing their willingness to sacrifice everything, even their lives, for one man, Adolf Hitler.

It was a sacrifice that Louise hoped she would never have to make. But she was prepared to do so if necessary.

'I didn't like the words of the oath. I felt uncomfortable saying them. But I did say them and, at the time, I meant them. I was young, I was patriotic and even though I was concerned about the course Germany was taking, the years of being brainwashed about the greatness of Hitler still had great influence over me. I truly believed I should serve my country, and if the war and the Nazis were the way to do that, then I would support both as fully as possible. Would I have died for Hitler? Perhaps. I don't think it would have been for him, but I would have sacrificed myself for Germany at that time. Later on, when the war had taken its toll, my level of idealism was far less. By 1945, my willingness to die for Germany was certainly not so great. I was too busy trying to stay alive.'

Louise quickly settled into her new role with Division 24, work which she found to be undemanding and pedestrian, but preferable to those monotonous days at the handbasin factory.

'My role was basically military administration, making reports, recording what sort of military supplies were needed. I had to do shorthand and typing and answering the phone as well. I was a much faster than average typist. I composed lists of how many cannons had been fired and how much ammunition had been used during practice. I wrote requests from the commandant for more weapons, more supplies from HQ in Hamburg. We never got as much as we wanted though — even in those early days of the war. Of course, later, shortages would become even more acute.'

Her work colleagues — predominantly men — were mostly civilians like herself. There were no uniforms and the rigid hierarchy of a conventional military office was distinctly lacking most of the time.

'The majority of the people that I worked with were told to join up, just like me. There were men with health problems that meant they couldn't go and fight and there were older men, some who'd already served in the First World War. Over time, I got to know the heads of the division. They were mostly older, professional soldiers. They were very disciplined, very Prussian in their manner. We respected that.'

Discussing details of their individual roles or even the war effort in general was forbidden.

'It was a fairly social sort of atmosphere in the first six months or so of the war, but we didn't sit around and gossip about our work. Initially, there was a sense of adventure about the whole business. Remember, most of us had been torn from our usual lives to do this work. It was something new, and I was quite excited by it all. It was the older men with previous military experience who really kept the atmosphere calm and more like a traditional military unit. Otherwise, I think those who had until recently been civilians would have probably chatted and laughed more — acted more like colleagues in an ordinary office environment. But the experienced military people kept us in line, and we quickly settled into a fairly dull routine. Most of the work we did was not that interesting anyway, and we had been told to keep the information we did know secret. No one would have risked being informed on.'

By 1941 the fairly relaxed pace of the office had intensified. The official working week — 8 am to 6 pm, six days a week — was becoming something of a distant memory as Division 24 struggled to maintain supplies to troops on an increasing number of fronts.

'Our workload gradually got bigger. Probably the busiest time I remember was during the African campaign. We were responsible for organising shiploads of vehicles and artillery to Rommel in the desert. We all worked overtime for weeks and weeks.'

Despite the mounting workload, Louise remembers her time at Division 24 with some fondness.

'It was quite a good job really. I got paid a lot more, which I appreciated of course. It was good to have a bit more money, even if there were less and less things available to spend it on. The people I worked with were nice enough, although I can't say I made many lasting friendships out of it. I think everyone still regarded the work as temporary, that before too long the war would be over and we'd all get back to our normal lives. People chatted and were friendly, but we were busy and the work seemed so serious that solid relationships with others didn't happen all that much. In the back of my mind though, what I really liked about the job was the possibility of a transfer. Wismar was a small town, a provincial place. I wanted to see more of the world. I wanted to get away from my mother. I knew working for the air force would be my best chance of getting out.'

The burden of an escalating war effort began to press more heavily on Wismar. Rations were tightened; meat and luxury goods became scarce; disgruntled queues began to form in stores.

'At first, the number of coupons given remained the same. The problem was that you might have a coupon for meat, but there was none available in the shops. So you had a useless coupon and no meat for dinner. By late 1941 even common things like vegetables were getting harder to find.'

Some of the recipes that have been preserved from the era reflect both the ingenuity of a hungry populace and the desperate food supply problems they confronted. Kartoffelpuffers, potato pieces and peels deep fried, grilled pigeon (free if you could catch one) and beetroot pudding — an odd marriage of sugar and grated beetroot baked in a pie, were all common wartime dishes. For sheer wishful thinking, a recipe for mock goose is worthy of mention. It consists in fact of potatoes, cheese and apples with nary a goose in sight.[7]

Louise never sampled the delights of mock goose, but she does recall the monotony of a rationed diet.

'Vegetables were the mainstay — they were the most commonly available thing. We could do wonders with a potato — boiled, fried or mashed. I remember the deep-fried potato peels, too. They actually weren't that bad if you were hungry enough. Of course, nobody in Wismar was starving at this point — people still had enough food to survive on. But it was very hard and some became quite depressed about it all. I had some meals in the Luftwaffe canteen, so I was luckier than most. These were usually better than anything we could get at home.'

Such was the severity of food shortages and the level of public discontent that by March 1942 Goebbels was compelled to justify continued cuts to the rationing program, blaming recent frosts for the lack of potatoes and claiming that the British people were in fact suffering far worse conditions. He also stated his determination to put an end to the flourishing black market.

> During war, all goods and foodstuffs belong to the whole nation. They must be distributed fairly. He who signs against this principle harms the community. Black marketeering, bribery, bartering or excessive prices will be punished. In serious cases, property will be seized or the death penalty imposed.[8]

1940 had seen the start of the Allied aerial bombing campaign. Hitler was particularly concerned about the threat of direct bombing attacks from the ocean and some 950 of the 3000 purpose-built air-raid shelters in Nazi Germany were located along and around the north German coastline. Although not yet directly in the bombers' sights, Wismar lay in the flight path for many of these raids. Air-raid sirens quickly became a harrowing fact of life for the local population.

The terror and utter helplessness felt during those hours when the sirens screeched out their warning and the sky above became the enemy is still clearly imprinted on Louise's memory.

'There were 12 air raids altogether when I was still living in Wismar. A couple of the air-raid shelters had actually been built before the war broke out, but we had been told they were to be used as storage. More lies. The bombers were generally on their way to somewhere else, usually Berlin. But we never knew for sure. Every time that siren went off you had to run for your life. You never knew whether a bomb was going to be dropped or not. You never knew if you were going to survive or not. Our apartment buildings had a cellar that had been converted into a shelter. The walls were reinforced. They kept water down there and some tools. The tools were meant to be used for digging our way out, in case we got buried in the shelter.

'We would sit down there just listening, not talking very much. It was very difficult, sitting and waiting and hoping for the best. There was nothing you could do except hope.

'People were affected very badly by the stress of it all. I remember people developed stomach ulcers or would just become very emotional all the time, even when there was no danger. It is not easy to live in fear.

'Some people suffered greatly. I had an aunt, for instance, who had six sons. Every one of them was killed during the war — one after another. In the end, she went mad and was locked up in an asylum.'

While the relationship between Louise and her mother remained as tense as ever during this period, the war had brought about a dramatic change in the dynamic of the Fox home.

Fritz Fox was drafted into the air force in early 1941 and, a few months later, Lucy was ordered to work as a tax consultant for several local businesses short-staffed because of the demand for manpower in the military.

'My father's role was as a musician in the air force, he was to be part of a military orchestra entertaining the troops around the country and also overseas. He was actually quite pleased to go. He was a man who loved culture, who had always wanted to see the world and experience new things. But his marriage had tied him down quite a bit and taken away that opportunity. In a funny sort of way I think he saw the war as an opportunity to do some of the things he had always wanted to.

'He got his wish too. From the day he left until the end of the war he only had the opportunity to come home once. And he travelled all through Germany and into Czechoslovakia and maybe other places too.

'When my mother was sent out to work as well, it left more responsibility for Gerda and me. Gerda was still at school at that stage. I think it also made my mother's life more interesting for her; she was busier and had less time to sit at home and complain. She finally started to give me more freedom. I was older, I was working and I think she just didn't have time to check up on me any more. The changes meant that our roles changed a little bit and we all had to help out more. Sometimes Gerda would make dinner; sometimes I would. Sometimes it was my mother. The three of us pooled our rations to try to get enough to eat. My days were very busy, there wasn't much time outside of work. I spent an hour a day just walking to work and back, although sometime I rode a pushbike. The three of us were all busy in our own jobs and our own routines. Of course, my mother and I still didn't get on, but there was less time to argue now.'

What little free time she had Louise tried to make as enjoyable as possible. She continued her weekly attendance at the German Sporting Club, a group she had been an active member of for many years. A purely recreational group with no political agenda, the club offered a welcome respite from the bellicose lecturing and Führer-worship offered at the compulsory German Girls' League meetings.

'It was an athletics club, nothing more. I did running, especially the 100-metre sprint which I loved, swimming, high jump, all of that. It was a mixed club, boys and girls. I made some lovely friendships with boys at the club, but I didn't have a real boyfriend. Of course, many of those boys were soon shipped away to the war. Many of them never came back. It's hard to know what happened to most of them; people lost touch with each other during the war. So while the Sporting Club was very enjoyable, it became sad to go each week and find another face missing from the group.'

With organised dances frowned upon and the usual social diversions of film and music strictly controlled by the government, there were few genuine, non-regulated amusements for Wismar's youth.

'There wasn't much to do, but then we didn't have a lot of free time anyway. We were forbidden dances; the government seemed to think that since there was a war on, nobody should have any fun. All our energies had to be preserved for the war effort, they told us — whatever that meant. But the Nazis couldn't stop private parties and even with rations, people would still hold them occasionally. There would be some music and we would tell jokes and try to relax. That was our fun.

'The air force gave me three weeks' vacation each year and I tried to make the most of my free time. In summer I would go with some girlfriends to one of the other towns on the Baltic Sea. We'd just swim and lie on the beach all day and try not to think too much about what was going on.'

In truth, any escape from the realties of wartime life could only be fleeting at best. As food shortages worsened, the number of absent friends increased and the fear of invasion loomed ever larger, Louise admits to occasions when she felt nothing but overwhelming despair, both for her own future and that of Germany itself.

'It was a difficult time. The air-raid sirens, hiding in the bunker, realising someone you had known all your life was at the front line — all those things were hard to take. The war was everywhere, you couldn't get away from it. The newspapers and the radio — all they talked about was victory and how well everything was going. I'd already started not to believe it. I coped by just shutting my mind to the whole thing as much as I could. It was never easy.'

In November 1942 Louise received her second set of directives from Luftwaffe HQ. She was to be transferred to Berlin the following week. Lucy Fox took the news badly — screaming abuse at her daughter for leaving Wismar. With her husband in the air force and

Gerda recently seconded to work as a domestic on short-staffed farms, Lucy was distressed and angry at the prospect of living through the war alone.

'She felt like everyone had left her behind, that she'd been abandoned by us. I think she was also upset at losing her housemaid — now there would be nobody to clean the house and she'd have to do it herself. She was very angry with me, but I didn't care. Orders were orders and there was nothing she could do about it. I packed my bag and got on the train to Berlin.'

At the age of 22 Louise Fox was finally getting out of Wismar and about to see something of the world.

'I was very excited. The train trip was around four hours and I spent the time wondering what Berlin would look like. I had of course never been there before. The orders were not very specific. They didn't tell me what my new job would be or even to where I would ultimately be transferred. I just had to be at a certain personnel office in Berlin at a certain time. I would be given further instructions then.

'I wasn't frightened at all. Berlin hadn't been bombed at that stage; that would come later. I had always been a very adventurous girl, even though I'd never really had an opportunity to do many adventurous things in Wismar. I was actually really happy to be going, I welcomed it. I felt like my life was finally starting to get interesting.'

The Berlin that greeted Louise on her arrival had changed dramatically since 1933. Before Hitler's Chancellorship, Berlin had laid claim to being one of the most influential cities in Europe. It was the second largest metropolis on the continent, a notable economic powerhouse that was also the major communications and transport hub of Central Europe. In terms of cultural influence, Berlin was rivalled only by Paris.

Since the early 1920s artists from around the world had been drawn to Berlin. Film-makers, architects, musicians, writers and painters were inspired by the energy of the city and its enthusiasm for the arts. The Swiss artist Paul Klee and the Russian Wassily Kandinsky staged joint exhibitions in the city, firmly establishing Berlin as the centre of the emerging avant garde movement. Alfred Doblin paid homage in his novel, *Berlin Alexanderplatz,* while Christopher Isherwood explored the city's decidedly decadent nightlife in his famous *Berlin Diaries.*

Berlin was regarded as the most hedonistic of the European capitals, a place where morality took a back seat to money. The city had a vibrant cabaret and night club scene, and was renowned as a mecca for homosexuals.

The Nazis however, were not amused. Once they were in power, galleries displaying modern art were closed, foreign artists and academics were vilified and pressured to leave the country, while new music, film and architecture were brought under Nazi control.

Bars and clubs deemed to attract undesirable elements such as socialists or Jews were shut down, and all homosexual bars and clubs were closed. The Eldorado, Berlin's most notorious such nightclub, was closed by the Nazis and, with ponderous irony, transformed into a propaganda centre.

By late 1942, the impositions of both war and National Socialism had left Berlin a chastened place. For Louise however, Berlin still had the ability to entrance.

'I was very impressed by Berlin. I thought it was wonderful. I loved the architecture and the excitement of being in a big city. It was still intact at that stage, the bombing raids hadn't begun.'

Her excitement was scarcely tempered by the news that she was to be based at the Luftwaffe Supreme Command in Potsdam, some 40 kilometres from Berlin.

'I was happy enough to learn that I was going to Potsdam. I knew working at the Supreme Command would be challenging, and I welcomed that. Potsdam had always been a very important place in the history of Germany. The Prussian kings had lived there, including

Frederick the Great. So I looked forward to seeing it. It was also still quite close to Berlin, so I knew I would have some opportunities to see the city in any case.'

Much as it is today, Potsdam was a city of ancient palaces, tranquil lakes and vast tracts of greenery. Parks and open spaces dominated the city, which in turn was encircled by heavily forested countryside. It was the perfect location for an important military base — close to Berlin, yet shielded from the gaze of aerial bombers by a canopy of trees.

Luftwaffe Supreme Command was located some seven kilometres from central Potsdam in a densely forested area called Wildpark, which had originally been home to Frederick the Great before the Hohenzollerns were toppled from the German throne.

While lacking the majesty of Frederick's vast Potsdam palace, the Supreme Command was an impressively large compound featuring a maze of administrative offices, barracks and bunkers, all painted in camouflage shades of brown and green. The side of a nearby hill had been turned into a vast bunker that housed the air force's telephone exchanges and was operated almost entirely by women. Wildpark was also the site of Goering's underground bunker, although the Luftwaffe commander was predominantly based in Berlin. Known as Kurfurst, the bunker could house up to 160 people and had enough supplies for around three months. It remains largely intact today.

While she had anticipated her new position would be demanding, even Louise was unprepared for the long hours and continual stress her work entailed.

'I was assigned to the Supply and Transport office, which had about 150 staff altogether. My section was air transport, meaning we had to supply planes to the front, Junkers 52, Heinkel He 111, Focke-Wulf-190 and so on. We calculated the number of planes lost and compared it to our current production.

'Our official working hours were long, seven days a week from nine in the morning until ten at night. But in reality, we usually worked much longer than that. Reports from the front lines usually starting coming in around midnight and we had to work through those, working out what the units needed and what we could provide. Most nights we would work through until two, three or even four in the morning and then have to be ready to start at nine again the next morning. The girls in my section didn't live at the base; we had accommodation in hotels in Potsdam. A bus would take us to and from work each day. But we didn't spend a lot of time in the hotels; usually we ended up sleeping in the office. It was exhausting; there was virtually no life outside of work.'

While much of the work was routine enough, there were occasions when even the shield of bureaucracy and form-filling was not sufficient to protect Louise from the very real human tragedy behind the war effort.

In late 1942, the German Sixth Army — more than a quarter of a million men — was encircled by the Russians near the Soviet city of Stalingrad. Insufficiently prepared for the bitter cold of a Russian winter, and already reduced to eating their own horses thanks to a daily ration of 50 grams of bread per man, the German troops had only one hope of salvation — an order from the Führer to withdraw. But Hitler, oblivious both to the impossibility of victory and the suffering of his men, refused to budge.

'It became vital to get supplies through to the men in Stalingrad — food, clothing, more weapons. But it was also increasingly difficult. We were short of all supplies, and getting them through proved very dangerous.

'The only way to get supplies in was by air. We'd already lost pilots trying to fly over the Russian lines and the situation was getting very grim. As the Stalingrad stand-off continued, I suppose some pilots realised it was a hopeless situation and they would simply get killed if they kept following orders to go into the area.

'One day I received an instruction to type up an order for execution. It was for six of our pilots. Apparently they had been caught tampering with their planes, creating mechanical problems so they would have an excuse not to fly out on their missions. They were to be executed by firing squad. I typed the order of course, but I will remember that day always. I don't think I cried, but I remember a terrible grimness and also some anger that young men should be treated like this.'

The Battle for Stalingrad would eventually claim more than 800,000 German men, a calamity from which Hitler's forces would never recover.

'Stalingrad was a farce. A terrible, terrible farce.' It was also the beginning of the end for the Nazi regime's insane tilt at power.

But the number of German defeats was not the only thing concerning the staff at Supreme Command. Increasingly frequent Allied bombing raids added to the tension.

'We had very unusual bunkers; they were pyramid-shaped buildings, built above ground. They were made of some special metal and were shaped so that the bombs would be deflected. They seemed to work okay. At first the sirens would only go off every couple of days, but it soon became far more frequent. Before long, it was every single morning and every single night. It was always the Americans in the daytime — they didn't like to fly in the dark — and the British at night.'

Perhaps it was the unrelenting stress of working in a war zone or perhaps it was simply a response to the inherent madness of the times, but life within the Supply and Transport division soon took on a surreal and slightly bacchanalian tone.

Drugs were dispensed morning and night to staff — 'A pill to put you to sleep and another to wake you up,' Louise recalls. 'I never asked exactly what was in the pills, but they seemed to work.'

Alcohol was not only allowed, but actively encouraged, and staff were free to drink at their desks as well as at their leisure.

'There was always alcohol available, French champagne, and good French cognac like Hennessy. I had the champagne mostly. Of course it all came from France, it was all stolen. Nobody ever said it out loud, but it was obvious. We didn't worry about that, it was the booty of war as far as we were concerned and we really needed something to get us through such long hours. Germany was at her peak in that time, we were on top of the world — or so we thought. Might is right. We drank our champagne and didn't think about where it came from.'

Even military uniforms were optional.

'We could choose whether or not to wear our uniform. Many of us did, especially since there were not many nice clothes available at the time because of the war. Our uniform was quite smart, a medium blue skirt and jacket with a gold eagle on one arm, signifying that we belonged to the air force.'

Despite such diversions, many staff succumbed to the constant pressure. Heated arguments became commonplace and weary officers often took out their fatigue on junior staff.

'There were some officers who shouted a lot, who were really hard on you if you made a mistake. We just had to accept that and try not to let it get on top of us too much — we knew that they were just as exhausted as we were. I was lucky; I had a number of aristocratic officers in my area, ones with the Von prefix to their name. Back then, those types of people were better educated and better mannered than the average person. They came from a different world, really. I always liked people from the upper classes; they were usually very charming.'

It's doubtful that blue-blooded Vons were very prevalent on Heinz Wolf's family tree. But Louise quickly decided she liked him very much in any case.

'One of my jobs every day was to relay messages to a pilot in another section of the Supreme Command. After a while we became more familiar with one another, chatting and so on if there was time. One day he mentioned that his mother was ill in hospital in Berlin and he would like to have some flowers for her. But flowers were impossible to get in Berlin — such things were simply not important during a war.

'We both knew that Supreme Command could obtain virtually anything. So I was able to organise the flowers through the office and on one of my rare free afternoons, I caught the train to Berlin with the flowers. I met him there. From the moment we met, we liked each other.

'His name was Heinz Wolf. He was 24 years old, very tall, blue-eyed, very blond. I had always liked fair men, I suppose because they looked so different to me — the attraction of opposites.'

The relationship between Louise and Heinz was passionate and intense. For a fortnight they stole whatever scant time they had to be together, always wishing the war away, but knowing that both love and life were fragile states in such turbulent times.

The two shared a love of culture, particularly music and art, and had long conversations dissecting favourite arias or musing over the finer points of some beloved painting.

'We had a lot in common. He hadn't finished his studies; the war had interrupted them. He had been planning to go to university to study art history. He still intended to go as soon as the war was over. But most important, he was nice to be with. He made me laugh.'

Propriety is always one of the first casualties of crisis. After two weeks together, and with Heinz scheduled to return to the dangerous skies over Germany, the couple decided to get married.

'Of course, you would never have married after a fortnight if it wasn't for the war. War changes everything, even romance. We didn't know what might happen tomorrow, there was no way of knowing. It made sense to marry while we could, and to worry about the consequences later. People act differently when they don't know how much time they have left.'

The couple became husband and wife in a brief civil ceremony conducted at Potsdam HQ. A church service was out of the question.

'Hitler didn't like organised religion much. It was frowned upon to go to church if you were a Party member. So, we played it safe. Besides, getting married where we worked was quick and simple. We didn't want to waste time with elaborate plans and suchlike.'

Sadly for Heinz, time was almost up. He was shot down and killed over Germany less than two weeks after his hasty wedding. When a telegram was delivered to Mrs Louise Wolf at Supreme Headquarters, she accepted it with trembling hands and an anguished heart, knowing what message it would contain.

'I was in very great shock. Of course, you know that there is danger, and being a fighter pilot, his job was more dangerous than most. But still, when the news comes, it is never expected. I remember thinking that it all seemed so unfair. He was young, he was intelligent, and he had so much to live for. Now he was gone.

'I believe my work saved me. I was given no time off to mourn; I was expected to continue working as usual. There was not much time to cry. I had to shut my mind to his death and just get on with it.'

Despite her stoicism, the pain of a life cut short and a relationship that was never permitted to reach its potential continued to haunt Louise for some years.

'Of course I wondered what might have happened had Heinz survived the war. Would we have lasted as a couple? Could we have survived the hardships of life in Germany once the war was over? I don't know. We didn't know each other very well really, it would have taken time to get used to each other, to discover whether we were a good match or not. Either way, my life would have probably been very different. But we can't know the future. And I realised after some time that it was futile to dwell on it.'

One of the few periods of respite allowed Supreme Headquarters staff was a three-hour lunch break. Offered in lieu of the long hours spent toiling through the night, the extended lunchtime gave Louise the opportunity for exercise and fresh air.

'Wildpark was surrounded by beautiful forests. It was actually a lovely part of the country. I always made the most of any free time I had. In summer, we would go swimming in the lake. In winter, even when it snowed, I would go for a walk or take a bicycle for a ride though the forest. It was my only chance to get some fresh air and to stretch my legs.'

One quiet cycle through the Wildpark greenery would have very unexpected consequences, however. On a particularly fine summer's day, Louise was riding along one of the numerous dirt tracks that criss-crossed the forest floor. Suddenly, from the corner of her eye, she noticed a sudden movement in some undergrowth by the side of the road. Thinking it was one of the wild deer that populated the park, Louise was about to ride on by when a man emerged from the bushes. He was wearing a British officer's uniform and pointing a gun squarely at Louise.

'I got such a shock that I fell off my bike. I scrambled to my feet and quickly drew out my own gun. I pointed it right back at him. Then we just stood there for a moment, staring at each other, both afraid to make a move. Just like in a bad film. I was looking at the first British person I had ever seen in my life. Finally, he spoke. 'Don't shoot,' he said. Thankfully, I had learnt English at school so I under-stood what he said. Gradually, we both lowered our guns a little, until finally they were both pointing at the ground. He started trying to explain to me who he was and how he got there. Apparently he was a pilot and his plane had been shot down. He had ejected and walked through the forest. His crew were still missing. Then I remembered that we'd been told about a missing British aircraft a few days before and warned to be on the lookout for the crew. And I had found one of them.

'I was relieved that he wasn't going to shoot me, but then I got really angry about the position he had put me in. There were always Luftwaffe staff walking about in these woods. What if someone had seen me? Here I was, standing with an enemy soldier, and I had lowered my gun and was even talking to him in a combination of

English, a little French, which he also understood, and some German. This was war, these were harsh times. I could have been charged with collaborating with the enemy. I would have been shot in the head.

'I got back on my bike and made him understand that he was to follow me. I didn't even ask for his gun. I rode ahead and he just followed me like a puppy. Before long, I came across a guard post. I called out to the guards, 'Look what I found'. They were amazed. They ran to the officer, took away his gun, and marched him away. I never saw him again. He was a good-looking man too, and I did feel sorry for him. I always hoped that he survived being taken prisoner of war and that he returned to England and had a happy life. Of course, there's no way of ever knowing the truth.

'I don't feel guilty about turning him in; he was the enemy and I would have been killed myself if I had been discovered letting him go. I like to think in some ways I may have saved his life. He'd obviously been out in the forest for some days, he would have been tired and hungry and scared. He could not have survived for long on the run. At least, by being a prisoner he had some chance of being fed. That's why he was so docile, why he just followed me. He knew it was the only chance he had left.'

A few days after the incident with the British airman, Louise was informed that the Luftwaffe Commander, Hermann Goering, was visiting Potsdam HQ and had asked to see her.

'The first thing I thought was — what have I done? I couldn't think of any major mistakes I had made, certainly not enough to attract Goering's attention. But I could not think why he would want to see me. I had been promoted to captain a little earlier, which was a reasonably high rank for a woman, but I certainly wasn't of any great importance to the Luftwaffe. The promotion wasn't really for any outstanding achievement; the Luftwaffe had a policy of regular promotions for those who were doing a good job. I suppose they thought we needed an incentive for all our hard work.

'Goering had not visited our offices in the year I had been there, so although I was nervous, I was also curious to meet him. He had a very big reputation in Germany; he was one of the few of Hitler's top men who was admired by most Germans. He had been a famous fighter pilot in the First World War, and he came from a noble family.'

Louise's first impressions of Goering were of a man larger than life, the sort of person who unselfconsciously dominates a room with his mere presence.

'He was big man, fat really I suppose, but tall and broad-shouldered with it. He immediately struck me as being very friendly. He had a broad smile and was very polite to me. He congratulated me for capturing the airman and for being so courageous. He then handed me a medal for bravery.

'I accepted it of course, but I knew it was not deserved. I hadn't been brave at all, I had fallen off my bike with fright, for heaven's sake. Still, there was no point in telling anyone else that.'

Later that same week, Louise was again called to Goering's office.

' "Miss Fox, I have decided that you are to come and work in my office in Berlin for a while," he said. And that was that. Apparently, one of his regular secretaries was ill and he was short staffed. He needed a replacement, and I had caught his eye.'

Two days later, Captain Louise Fox was back on the fast train to Berlin, going to work for the second most powerful man in Germany.

4 HERMANN GOERING'S SECRETARY

> *'I am what I have always been: the last Renaissance man, if I may be allowed to say so.'*
>
> Reich Marshall Hermann Goering at Nuremberg.

EVERY CRIME, regardless of its nature, stems from one of two prime motivators. The first is the desire for profit, the second is in response to passion. We kill for money or vengeance, we steal out of greed or envy. Crime is either a means of obtaining what should not be rightfully ours, or the final expression of an overriding emotional urge.

For the majority of Hitler's top-ranking men, the crimes they committed in the name of National Socialism were inspired by a fervent belief in both the righteousness of the cause and the infallibility of their Führer.

The pugnacious and abrasive Ernst Roehm, his face horribly scarred from combat in the First World War and his body bloated from the effects of a rabidly hedonistic lifestyle, was both mentor and confidant of Hitler from the early days of the German Workers Party. He still regarded the Führer as his friend, right up until the moment Hitler ordered he be shot in the head for alleged treason in 1934. Heinrich Himmler, head of the notorious SS, was an underachieving fertiliser salesman until he joined the Nazi ranks. He used his fanatical devotion to his leader as a shield against much of the horror and human suffering perpetrated under his leadership. Watching the execution of Jewish 'spies and saboteurs' in Minsk, Belorussia, during the early years of the war, Himmler is reported to have turned green and begun to shake as a bedraggled group of terrified young men, women and children were shot as they lay face down in a purpose-built trench. When the firing stopped, however, he reminded his soldiers of their duty to Germany and the Führer, urging them to continue, no matter how 'hideous and frightful' their orders might seem.[1]

Rudolf Hess, Deputy Führer at the height of his influence, made his feelings clear in a 1934 address to the nation. 'Through your oath you bind yourself to a man who — that is our faith — was sent to us by higher powers. Do not seek Adolf Hitler with your mind. You will find him through the strength of your hearts.'[2] A few years later at Nuremberg, frail and increasingly incapacitated by bouts of neurosis and delusion, Hess was able to gather together the tangled threads of his sanity just long enough to defend the indefensible. 'I regret nothing,' he told his captors, adding that be expected to find a reward in Heaven for the role he had played in promoting the Nazi cause.

There was no more obsessive admirer of Hitler than Joseph Goebbels. The man who spent his time as Nazi propaganda minister, convincing the multitudes of the Führer's greatness, needed no such convincing himself. His extensive diaries, published in full after the war, reveal a level of obsequiousness not for the faint-hearted.

'I love him. Such a sparkling mind has my leader. I bow to the greater man, to the political genius,' goes a typical entry from the early 1930s.[3]

Indeed, so notorious was Goebbels' depth of feeling for Hitler amongst the Nazi rank and file that rumours persisted of a homosexual relationship between the two, despite Goebbels' persistent and well-publicised womanising. Indeed, there is ample evidence to suggest that Goebbels abandoned a torrid affair with a movie actress and returned to his long-suffering wife Magda in an effort to please the Führer, who had long admired Mrs Goebbels' wit and dogged allegiance to the Party.

Despite their markedly different backgrounds and personalities, Roehm, Hess, Himmler and Goebbels were all fawning acolytes, shadows of men who thought what Hitler thought, agreed with his every notion and spent their brief careers devising ever more Machiavellian plans to win his favour and oust their rivals in the battle for the Führer's affection. Nazism was far more than a means of obtaining power; it was a quasi-religious philosophy, a bizarre mish-mash of Nordic folklore, anti-Semitism, pseudo-science and militarism that they desperately believed represented the only true future for Germany and for themselves.

Based on the time she spent working with him, Louise remains convinced, after 60 years, that Hermann Goering was a man of a very different calibre from his contemporaries.

One senses a degree of internal conflict when Louise discusses her views on her former boss. It is clear that, at times, she still struggles to reconcile the wise-cracking, charismatic man she knew with the reality of his role in the Nazi regime and the myriad atrocities committed in its name. Like the person who discovers his kindly next-door neighbour is a serial killer, Louise appears to hate what Goering represented, but finds it difficult to hate the man himself.

'To be truthful, I liked him. He had charisma and he was very stylish. Goering was a larger-than-life sort of character; he always stood out from everyone else around him. He had been wealthy and privileged all his life, really, and it showed in his manner and his personality. He was confident, he gave the impression of being someone who was used to getting his own way all the time. When Goering spoke, people listened. And not only because he was their commanding officer. He was engaging. All the staff liked him, and there were not many very senior officers that we did like. Most of them were very demanding, and the stress of the war made them aggressive and unreasonable a lot of the time. Goering could get very angry. He had a temper, that's for sure — but he reserved it for people higher up than me. He was usually very kind to his office staff.

'He was very large and quite fair. He was a hard-drinking man, and he liked to eat fine foods. But so did virtually every other officer I knew — apart from Hitler, of course. There were a lot of big drinkers and eaters back then. People overindulged whenever they could. Goering, I would say, was one of the worst, but he certainly wasn't the only one. He could drink an enormous amount — he would often drink heavily while he was at his desk working — but it rarely seemed to slow him down. He could hold his alcohol, that's for sure. I never heard him slur his words or appear really intoxicated, but I know on many occasions he had been drinking solidly for several hours.

'To an extent, alcohol was part of that military culture. As I have said before, drinking was actually encouraged and almost everyone did it. Goering drinking whiskey or cognac while he was working was not looked on as something he shouldn't be doing. Nobody thought much of it, really.

'He had a loud voice, one of those booming voices that carries across a room. It had a jolly sound to it most of the time. Goering was without doubt the friendliest high-ranking officer I ever met. He had a good sense of humour and would tell us jokes all the time. Well, perhaps not jokes really, more like little funny or encouraging remarks. He didn't tell us the normal sort of jokes that have a punch line; it was more his manner of speaking to us. He was usually very positive and always had a smile for everyone. He was good for our morale, actually. I did feel quite appreciated when he took the time to say thank-you or please to me. Most senior officers would not bother with something like that. He laughed a lot, even though he was under a great deal of pressure. He was a very hard worker; we did admire him for that. Even with his drinking, he seemed to get a lot done. He worked the same long hours as us; he started early in the morning and would work way past midnight most of the time.'

Despite presenting himself as the very model of unwavering obedience to the Nazi cause, Louise has no doubts that Goering was a man much more concerned with his own wellbeing than any hollow ideology.

'Goering was all about power in my opinion. It was obvious that he thrived on being in charge, on being a leader. I think he would have jumped on any cause, on any agenda if he thought it would put him in a position of power. It just so happened that Hitler came along, and Goering took advantage of that.

'It's just my view, but I really don't believe that Goering cared all that much for some of Hitler's policies. The treatment of the Jews, the concentration camps, I think it was Hitler who really believed in those things. To Goering, I think they were a means to an end. In some ways that makes him even worse than Hitler. Hitler was a madman, but Goering certainly wasn't. He knew exactly what he was doing, And he didn't care who died, who was hurt, or what terrible damage was inflicted on Germany and the German people. He just wanted power.'

Goering's own comments and much of his own behaviour during critical periods of the war indicate that Louise's intuition may be near the mark.

'I joined the party because I was a revolutionary, not because of any ideological nonsense,' he told the jurors at Nuremberg, and while it is easy to assume he was merely excusing himself from the excesses of Nazi social policy, the truth is his role within the Party had always been solidly grounded in pragmatism.[4]

Born in Rosenheim, Bavaria in 1893, Goering was the product of an upper middle class family. His father, Dr Heinrich Goering, was a career diplomat who had played a key role in the German colonisation of Namibia before the First World War and was an enthusiastic German imperialist. His mother, Fanny Tiefenbrunn, was Dr Goering's second wife, a sturdy blonde almost 20 years her husband's junior. Their marriage had caused a minor social scandal, with rumours abounding that the widowed Dr Goering placed the decidedly working-class Miss Tiefenbrunn in the family way long before they decided to walk down the aisle. Whatever the truth, the newly married Goerings fled to remote south-west Africa to escape further public scrutiny. Four children from Dr Goering's first marriage were left behind in the care of relatives. It is understood their father never saw them again.

The Goerings remained abroad for five years, during which time they had three children. With the impending birth of a fourth, they opted to return to Germany for the birth. Hermann Goering would later boast that such was his mother's patriotic fervour for Germany that she had travelled all the way from Africa just to ensure he was born on German soil. His thoughts on the fact that she then returned to Africa with her husband, leaving her new infant son with family for the next three years, are not known. Armchair psychologists however, might make much of the fact that children who are abandoned in their formative years often grow into attention-seeking and rather manipulative adults.

Whilst overseas, the Goerings had befriended a Jewish-Austrian doctor called Hermann Epenstein. Later, when the Goerings returned to Munich permanently, Epenstein — now officially Ritter (Knight) von Epenstein after donating vast sums of money to the Austrian royal court — became a frequent visitor, and within a short time, Fanny Tiefenbrunn became his mistress.

Epenstein was an extremely wealthy man, and one of his most prized possessions was a magnificent castle at Veldenstein, near modern-day Nuremberg. The Goering clan would regularly spend long holidays at the castle, a wondrously gothic structure perched atop a jagged cliff that overlooked the Pegnitz River. Young Hermann loved the sheer pageantry and opulence of his borrowed surrounds, just as he formed a very close bond with Epenstein himself, whose wealth, extravagance and vitality were in marked contrast to the character of his cautious and rather submissive father. Over time, the affair between their host and their mother became an open family secret, and in his final years, Dr Goering was forced to occupy a small cottage on the edge of the estate while his wife and children holidayed in the castle. The fact that Fanny's final child, Albert, was the only dark-haired sibling amongst a brood of blue-eyed blonds, and bore an uncanny resemblance to Dr Epenstein, was accepted without comment.

This unconventional if rather confused upbringing set the tone for the rest of Goering's life. The possessor of a raw native cunning rather than any great intellect, Goering grew into a handsome if rather bombastic young man, popular in the moneyed social circles that the Epenstein connection had given him entrée to. Naturally egotistical and almost comically vain, the fame he attracted with his fighter pilot exploits during the First World War only served to convince Goering further of his own greatness. A talented and fearless pilot, he flew several missions with the 'Red Baron', Manfred von Richthofen and later earned the Pour le Mérite, Germany's highest military decoration. By the war's end, Goering was undoubtedly one of the most famous soldiers in Germany. His picture appeared in countless newspapers, he was profiled in several national magazines and a series of commemorative postcards, featuring a suitably brooding Goering wearing his medal, sold very well.

By 1919 however, the German appetite for military heroes had understandably waned.

Slightly used flying aces were no longer in demand. Worse still from Goering's perspective, gangs of Bolsheviks roamed the city streets often heckling and sometimes attacking any returned soldiers still wearing their uniforms. Goering himself almost lost one of his prized medals in a Munich street scuffle.

When the newly installed Ebert government tried to bring in legislation forbidding returned servicemen from wearing all their finery in public, Goering could remain silent no longer. He helped organise a large demonstration against the new laws and made a rousing speech attacking the new government. Naturally, he wore full dress uniform, resplendent with medals and insignia.

> For four long years we officers did our duty and risked our lives
> for the Fatherland. Now we come home and how do they treat
> us? They spit on us and deprive us of what we gloried in
> wearing. And therefore I ask everyone here tonight to cherish
> hatred, a deep and abiding hatred of those swine who have
> outraged the German people and our traditions. But the day will
> come when we drive them out of our Germany. Prepare for that
> day. Arm yourselves for that day. Work for that day. It will surely
> come.[5]

Disillusioned with Germany, Goering, now twenty-six years old, used the remnants of his fame to secure a number of lucrative overseas positions, working as a stunt pilot in Stockholm and an aircraft adviser to the Danish government. It was during this time he met and fell desperately in love with Carin von Kantzow, the daughter of an aristocratic Swedish colonel and the wife of a wealthy Stockholm-based businessman. Von Kantzow quickly divorced her husband and the pair, together with her son, returned to Munich in 1922, just as the city was abuzz with talk of a radical new political party — the National Socialist German Workers' Party.

Goering first encountered Adolf Hitler in November of that same year, after Hitler had addressed a mass street demonstration. Although he was impressed and somewhat intrigued by Hitler the man, even in those early days, Goering saw the Party as a means to achieving personal power and Hitler as merely a conduit to that end.

'I hated the Republic,' he said during one his Nuremberg interviews. 'I knew it would not last. I saw that as soon as the Allies withdrew their support, a new government would take over Germany. I wanted to help destroy the Republic and to be, perhaps, the ruler of the new Reich.'[6]

He would later claim that Hitler actually agreed at their very first meeting that Goering should become leader once they had seized power. The veracity of that claim is difficult to gauge, given Goering's pomposity and tendency to exaggerate, but there is no doubt that Hitler, delighted to have a high-profile war hero on side, unhesitatingly offered the politically inexperienced Goering an important role within the party, putting him in charge of the SA.

Despite his many character flaws, Goering was an extremely hard worker when motivated, and he quickly played a pivotal role in raising the Nazi profile, calling on his well-heeled friends as well as his new wife's European connections.

It is significant that of all the players in the Nazi saga, Goering was one of the few of independent means (although bad business deals and a fondness for extravagance meant that Goering regularly both made and lost fortunes), and the only one who enjoyed a high public profile before 1933. It could be said that, at least in those early years, the Nazi Party needed Hermann Goering far more than he needed it. While there is no doubt that he wholeheartedly supported many of Hitler's key policies, particularly the imperialistic notion of Lebensraum, Goering had no prior history of anti-Semitism and no interest in eugenics. In fact, given his regard for his mother's long-time lover, the half-Jewish Dr Epenstein, it is difficult to place him in the same category as Goebbels, Himmler and Bormann, Hitler's most fervent haters of Jews.

Indeed, there is ample anecdotal evidence of Goering personally intervening on several occasions to save the lives of Jews who had some prior relationship with his family. It is also believed that he colluded with his younger, Austrian-based brother Albert (who may well have been partly Jewish himself) to allow several Jewish families to escape Vienna.

But there is no doubt that Hermann Goering both knew of and played a significant role in the deaths of millions of Jews and other racial and political minorities, while having no particularly intense personal hatred for them. Although he had vigorously opposed the Kristallnacht pogrom in 1938, he had done so on economic rather than moral grounds. Goering did not oppose the Nuremberg Laws and indeed spoke several times in their defence, on one occasion telling the Reichstag that if God had wanted all men to be equal he would not have created different races.

As Minister for Economic Affairs, he gifted himself with the state-owned Hermann Goering Works — a stolen industrial complex employing some 700,000 workers (mostly drawn from concentration camps) and with a capital base of more than 400 million marks. His lavish lifestyle was largely funded by money he extracted illegally from German-owned industries under his control. Goering also directed the forced labour programs in the occupied territories under which hundreds of thousands of people were brutalised, starved and eventually killed. He supported their demise simply as a means of advancing his own place in the Nazi regime and lining his own pockets. Self-interest drove Goering's every move; his passion for the Nazi Party was a mere flicker compared to the roaring fire of his own ambitions.

By the time Louise found herself in the unexpected position of being his secretary, time, tragedy and the pressure of running the Luftwaffe had taken their toil on Goering. His once attractive features were swollen from years of excessive drinking, and he was very overweight. Goering had survived a serious morphine addiction (which had arisen from treatment for an injury received during the Beer Hall Putsch) and the death of his beloved Carin from tuberculosis in 1931. Long one of Hitler's favourites, he was also coming under increasingly critical scrutiny as Germany's air campaign rapidly began to unravel.

'I saw Goering virtually every day when he was in Berlin. He had two main secretaries, me and another girl that I shared an office with.

'The Air Command headquarters was located on the Wilhelmstrasse, in the central part of Berlin. The offices were large and quite lavish. I remember beautiful carpets, nice furniture and lovely curtains. It was a nice environment, the same as Potsdam, perhaps even nicer. It was quite bizarre I suppose to have such luxury in the middle of a war, but I certainly wasn't complaining. If anyone thought it was immoral or unfair, I certainly didn't hear them say so. I think the air force wanted to make up for the long hours we were expected to work. It was an incentive, and it certainly worked. It was a crazy way to live, really. Outside the office, everyone was suffering. Food was scarce; life was hard and dangerous. People were losing loved ones by the thousands. Inside the office though was like being in a sort of cocoon. The hard work stopped you thinking too much about what was going on outside. You drank, ate chocolate and tried to forget what was really happening.

'There was the same access to alcohol, pills and good food in the Berlin office. We ate and drank things that most people hadn't seen for several years. And it was always top quality, too — only the very best. Goering had a constant stream of generals and high-ranking officials waiting to see him, and often they had to wait for some time. One of my tasks was to see they had plenty to eat and drink while they waited. Cognac, fresh fruit, champagne — we had it all. I can't remember too many of them ever saying no, either. Sometimes — if they had been away from Berlin for quite some time — they would look quite amazed when I came out with all these drinks and fresh food. It must have looked like heaven to them. Others, mostly those who never went out into the field themselves, were used to such things. But everyone indulged in whatever was offered. I guess in the back of their minds they were wondering how long this could all last.

Despite being a little overawed by not only Goering himself but the constant parade of high-ranking Luftwaffe officers that passed through the office, Louise quickly found her feet in Berlin.

'I was a little bit nervous when I first started, mainly because I was surrounded by so many really high-ranking people. That was a little intimidating. And that atmosphere was intense and sometimes aggressive, but I was used to that by now. It didn't worry me too much. The secret was to keep your head down and work hard.

'I settled in very quickly, especially after I'd met Goering and realised he was actually quite good to work for. I'd been reading about him of course, even before the war; he was well known. I remembered the newspaper articles about his magnificent wedding in Berlin, when he married his second wife, the actress Emmy Sonnemann. She was very popular in Germany at the time too. Together they were a very high-profile couple. I never saw her though. It wouldn't have been that common for the commander's wives to visit the office anyway, unless for a social function or something like that. So, for me, working for Goering at first was a bit like working for a celebrity. Except, of course, he was much more powerful than any normal celebrity.'

In fact Goering's power was so great that Louise could have been imprisoned without trial or even executed on a single word from her commander. That she was now keeping very dangerous company was a fact that had not escaped her, but one which she managed to put into perspective.

'It was true of course that Goering and the others with high rank had the power of life and death over us. But I had become used to it. It wasn't the sort of thing that you sat around thinking about each day. You would go mad if you did. And the reality is that someone like me was simply too unimportant to attract Goering's attention — unless I did something traitorous. We all knew what the rules were and nobody

I knew of personally ever tried to break them. I always did as I was told and kept my opinions mostly to myself. That was how I kept safe. Besides, I don't think we were in any more danger than the average person on the street who had to deal with SS thugs and such. Nobody was safe. And at least people like me served a purpose, we were useful in the eyes of those in charge.'

Goering's fondness for lavish uniforms and fancy dress (which for some years made him the target of many jokes — not all of them good natured — in Nazi circles) only added to his star appeal. Louise still vividly recalls how the solemnity of war had done little to persuade the Reich Marshall to revert to less showy attire.

'I never saw him look untidy, not once. He was a very elegant dresser and he seemed to take great pride in what he wore. He had lots of different uniforms, each one designed by him. They were based on various air force uniforms, but they weren't the usual issue. He had them modified in some way; they might be a different colour or have different decorations. He always wore very expensive material and the uniforms were very well cut. Goering's uniforms were always heavy with insignia and medals. He must have awarded himself every military medal in Germany, I think. Perhaps he even invented some medals just for himself.'

While Goering's vanity was obvious, Louise admits to finding it rather endearing at the time.

'Yes, we all knew he was very vain. He was a bit of a peacock really. He liked to strut around the office. I suppose a grown man worrying about his appearance so much — especially in the middle of a war — was silly. But I liked to see him dressed that way. He was an aristocratic man, back in the times when Germany still had real aristocrats. I didn't see anything wrong with it. He was, after all, very famous and very rich. Of course, now, looking back it's easy to laugh at him and say he was pompous. But when you were seeing him every day, he didn't appear that way at all.'

Louise's parents, Fritz and Lucy Fox.

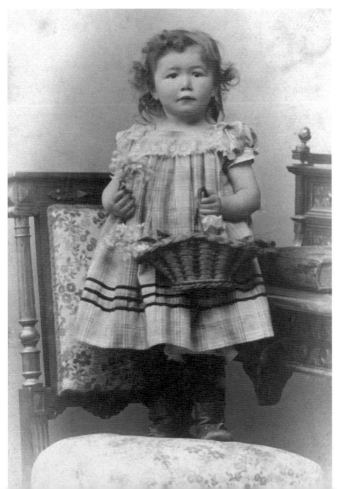

Louise as a small girl in Wismar.

The market square in Wismar in more recent times.

Louise as a
young woman.

Louise's colleagues outside the building
where they worked in Potsdam.

General Langemeier, Louise's commanding officer for a time.

Louise finds time for a break in her busy day, 1943.

General Langemeier is farewelled on his retirement, Goldap, 1944.

Fritz Fox in 1941, shortly after he was drafted into the air force.

Hermann Goering's hunting lodge in East Prussia, where Louise found unbelievable riches.

Louise (*sixth from right*) with her colleagues outside Kaiser Wilhelm's Hunting Lodge in East Prussia.

Left: Hermann Goering in full uniform before the war. (*Photo: Corbis*)

Below: Louise's final wartime workplace at Berchtesgaden, Bavaria.

Louise walks across the dykes at Cuxhaven after the war.

Louise reunited with her sister Gerda in Cuxhaven. In the background (*left*) is the building where Louise worked with the British Shipbuilding Control Commission.

Fritz and Lucy Fox in later life. Louise never saw them again after the war.

Louise in the 1950s, about to make the long journey to Australia.

Louise's sister, Gerda, who married an American and settled in the United States.

Ron Johnson, Louise's partner for over 20 years. He died in 1995.

Louise in later life in Australia, happy and settled at last.

In fact, the meticulousness of his workday attire paled into insignificance compared to some of the lavish and outlandish costumes he preferred for special occasions. When entertaining guests at Carinhall, the country estate named in honour of his first wife, Goering would often sport bizarrely remodelled Lederhosen and on more than one occasion greeted visitors wearing colourful medieval garb. Those long childhood summer days spent playing 'king' of Ritter Epenstein's castle were obviously still casting a spell over the adult Goering. When he presented himself to American forces for surrender in 1945, he brought along no fewer than 16 matching leather suitcases, a hatbox and his own valet. A subsequent medical examination found that his fingernails and toenails had been meticulously varnished.

Otto Gunsche, Hitler's personal assistant and Heinz Linge, his butler and the man charged with pouring petrol over the dead bodies of Hitler and Eva Braun after their suicides, were both captured and interrogated by the Russians in 1945. The transcripts of those lengthy interviews were discovered recently by two German historians searching through Soviet Secret Service documents in Moscow. Amongst the many revelations they contain about Hitler and his entourage is a reference to Goering and his reputation as a dandy and a braggart.

Gunsche was present when Goebbels shared the latest scurrilous rumour about Goering with the Führer over dinner. It seemed that Goering was alleged to have taken to wearing his medals to bed, pinning each one carefully onto his pyjamas each night.

According to Gunsche, Hitler roared with laughter and immediately told one of his assistants to 'order some medals made out of gold and silver foil along with a bombastic citation for bravery to be presented to Goering'.[7]

Mild-mannered with his support staff, Goering could, however, be a tough taskmaster to his Luftwaffe generals.

'We had generals coming in all the time for meetings with Goering. Most of the time these went normally enough, but there were times when he became very angry. I remember him screaming and shouting at one group of generals for a very long time, cursing them for their failure. The reality of course was that it wasn't their failure at all. We simply didn't have the supplies and the aircraft that they needed to carry out Goering's strategy.'

Louise's role at Goering's HQ primarily involved taking messages for her boss over the phone and then reporting that information to the Reich Marshall in the form of a typewritten report. The messages were always in code, a skill that Louise had mastered at Potsdam. While her role as messenger made her privy to a great deal of highly classified information, little of it made much sense removed from its context and none of it revealed to Louise the truth about the Luftwaffe's increasingly desperate situation.

'Receiving and writing messages in code probably sounds very exciting, but it wasn't really. Code was used for just about everything at that time, there was such paranoia about secrets leaking and information getting to the enemy. Some of the information I passed on may have been vital, but there was no way for me to know that really. Of course, I — like everyone else who worked with me — realised that our air force wasn't doing as well as the citizens were being told. But I only knew a fraction of what was really a much more complicated story.'

In fact, the German air force, initially the golden child of the armed services, was rapidly coming apart at the seams.

The Luftwaffe had enjoyed easy victories at the beginning of the war against less than formidable foes like Poland, Norway, Holland and Belgium. Had the Allies acted quickly in massing their own air forces together, even these outcomes might have been different. But Britain and France hesitated, allowing Goering's Luftwaffe to shine and overcome the very real numerical disadvantage they faced against the Allied forces.

Hitler was lulled into a false sense of confidence in the Luftwaffe's ability and strength, and Goering — who had been appointed Marshall of the Reich in July 1940 for his role in creating 'the preconditions for victory' — was content to allow the air force's weaknesses to remain hidden.

As the Allied attacks intensified, however, Goering found it increasingly difficult to paper over the cracks appearing in the Luftwaffe's performance. For a while he tried to bluff his way out of the impending crisis, issuing a flurry of false reports on the air force's strike and attrition rates.

In August 1940 for instance, German intelligence reported that 644 British aircraft had been destroyed in a single week of combat and 11 airfields permanently destroyed. In truth, the real figures were 103 downed aircraft and a single airfield only temporarily out of service. In that same year, the Germans lost an incredible 2630 aircraft (of which 1764 were totally destroyed) in less than three months. In September 1940 alone, 1000 aircraft were destroyed. By year's end, Germany was producing less than half the number of planes being produced by Britain, a handicap from which it was never able to recover.[8]

In the latter years of the conflict, Goering's preferred method of dealing with the Luftwaffe failure was to retreat to Carinhall, often for weeks at a time. There amidst the banquets and general frivolity he was able to ignore the ever-lengthening list of German air defeats, if only for a short time.

For those at the coal-face, like Louise, there was no lavish castle to seek refuge in. The grim reality of Germany's situation greeted them every day as they sat at their desks. But in spite of their inside knowledge, Louise and her colleagues preferred to cling to blind optimism for as long as possible.

'I only learned just how short of supplies and aircraft we had been for the entire war after it was all over. We only dealt with our little pieces of information; we never saw the whole picture. It wasn't even something that we discussed amongst ourselves for fear of getting caught and punished. Of course, there were times when I knew we were short of some particular item in one particular area because of the messages I had to pass on. But that wasn't enough to give the impression that we were being defeated more widely. Even working as we did, people in my position could only know what the government wanted us to. If they said we were winning, we believed we must be.'

It was on a weekday morning no less frantic than usual that Louise had her first direct contact with Adolf Hitler.

'I was working at my desk when suddenly the door to the office burst open. There was no knock. This man appeared and as I looked up — a little surprised that anyone should burst into Goering's offices without even knocking — I realised it was Hitler himself. I leapt to my feet and said Sieg Heil and gave the Nazi salute. Hitler glanced at me a moment and then just grunted. "Carry on," was all he said and he marched straight into Goering's office followed by a few other people. I did as I was told and went back to my typing.'

Coming face-to-face with the Führer left Louise feeling rather more underwhelmed than you might expect.

'You see, my dear, Hitler is known around the world today for the terrible thngs he did. He is infamous. And, of course, the day I met him he was the most powerful and famous man in Germany, too. But he didn't impress me all that much. Afterwards I thought how it was strange that such a powerful, important person could look so ordinary in the flesh. He was a little man, and there was certainly nothing very inspiring about his appearance. His skin was very pale, I remember that; too pale really. He had bags under his eyes. Goering at least looked like a leader. Hitler looked like an ordinary person in the street. He was a man you wouldn't have noticed at all in a crowd.

'Of course, I was surprised to see him standing in front of me. After all, I had been lectured about how wonderful he was since I was a child. Hitler was a big part of our lives then, whether we liked it or not. And yes, I was a little nervous too. But I wouldn't say I was in awe of him. I was old enough by then to know that he was just a man, not a god. I respected him at that time; this was before the war was lost and when I still believed that we had no choice but to go to war. But respect and admiration are two very different things. I can't say I admired him very much as a human being.'

Louise was not alone in her opinion. Adolf Hitler's grasp on the leadership of Germany may well have been beyond dispute at this time, but he had hardly won over the hearts and minds of the Nazi rank and file.

'He had a terrible reputation for being a difficult, angry man. He was always in a bad mood. He was in a terrible mood the day he burst into Goering's office, it was obvious. He looked angry and he also looked very tired. People were frightened of him, that was the sense I got from talking with others who had met him or worked around him for any period of time. People said he was generally unfriendly and hostile. Of course, this wasn't the sort of conversation you would have openly, but people would still whisper and talk when they felt comfortable doing so.

'One of my commanding officers at Potsdam, General Langemeier, later told me about a trip he had to Berlin where he and some other generals had a meeting with Hitler. The meeting did not go well and Hitler had flown into a terrible, uncontrolled rage. The General said to me, "Now I have seen it all. I saw Hitler get so angry that he went down on his knees and bit the carpet in front of all of us. I wanted to laugh, but I didn't dare — he was already mad enough."'

Immediately after the war a theory explaining Hitler's extreme moodiness emerged and gained widespread credence.

'The truth was that Hitler was not a well man,' Louise recalls. 'He didn't look well either time I saw him face-to-face — he visited the office twice during my time there, but on the second occasion he didn't even speak to me at all. His skin was the colour of chalk and he looked like he hadn't slept properly in days. However, I assumed that was just the result of the long hours he worked and all the stress. Later,

I was told that Hitler had syphilis. The story was that he had caught it from a Viennese prostitute — a Jewish one — and that his anger and wild behaviour were actually as a result of his disease. He was going mad, you see but, unfortunately for Germany, he was still in charge of the country. Nobody knew about his illness, of course. Can you imagine if something like that had become common knowledge? His own men were already trying to kill him — there were so many failed assassination attempts. If his sickness had been known, I don't think he could have stayed in power.'

Despite being an almost universally accepted truth in post-war Germany, the syphilis theory fell out of favour with historians soon after. An alternate proposal that suggested Hitler had Parkinson's disease rather than a venereal affliction later emerged as a more credible concept — based in part on witness accounts of Hitler's trembling hands and apparently semi-paralysed arm during his last days in the bunker. The notion that Hitler was simply bad rather than mad has also been widely discussed.

In recent years however, the idea that Hitler's erratic and maniacal behaviour may have been at least partially as a result of the brain degeneration typically symptomatic of late-stage syphilis has been increasingly re-examined. In her book *Pox: Genius, Madness and the Mysteries of Syphilis*, author Deborah Hayden makes a strong case in support of the syphilis connection based in part on the medical records of Hitler's personal physician, Dr Theodor Morell.

Morell, who oddly (and perhaps significantly) enough was a skin and venereal disease specialist in Berlin before being appointed to tend the Führer, kept meticulous daily records of the symptoms experienced by and the treatment given to his very special patient. According to those records, Hitler continually experienced an irregular heartbeat, tremors and suffered intermittently from encephalitis, dizziness, neck pustules, angina-like chest pains and lesions on his shins so painful that he was sometimes unable to wear boots. All of these are textbook signals of end-stage syphilis. Moreover, the doctor's preferred treatment was daily injections of iodide salts, at the time the most widely accepted treatment for syphilis. He also supplied his patient with large and regular doses of highly addictive methamphetamines, which he referred to as multivitamins, as well as cocaine eye drops for a persistent infection in Hitler's right eye.

While the syphilis theory will undoubtedly never be proven beyond doubt, it does offer a plausible explanation for Hitler's disinterest in sexual relations with women (although adherents of the Hitler-as-secret-homosexual theory may offer an alternative explanation for this aspect of his personal life) and provides insight into why he devoted a full thirteen pages of *Mein Kampf* to the subject of eradicating syphilis.

'The question of combating syphilis should have been made to appear as the task of a nation,' he wrote, adding, perhaps unsurprisingly, that the spread of the disease could be traced back to the Jewish population.[9]

It would also explain his irrational outbursts, his megalomania — even why the leader of one of Europe's largest nations would bite carpet in front of his assembled generals. Paranoia, uncontrollable anger and a dulling of the moral senses are all recognised symptoms of the disease.

Albert Speer, the architect who became Hitler's Armaments Minister, noted the Führer's rapid physical and mental decline during a visit to the Berlin bunker in 1945.

'Now, he was shrivelling up like an old man. His limbs trembled, he walked stooped with dragging footsteps. Even his voice became quavering and less masterful. His complexion was sallow, his face swollen, his uniform which in the past he had kept scrupulously neat was often neglected ... and stained by food he had eaten with a shaking hand ... he continued to commit nonexistent divisions or to order units supplied by planes that could no longer fly for lack of fuel ...'[10]

At the time of Speer's farewell visit, Adolf Hitler was 56 years old.

People who can claim to have met Adolf Hitler face-to-face belong to a small and rather exclusive club. For Louise Fox, her encounter has served to remind her that history is often more myth than fact.

'Hitler has been portrayed as an evil genius. He's become a comic-book character, larger and more horrible than a real person could ever be. But to me, he was a little, sickly Austrian man who perhaps started out with good intentions, but then went off the rails. You don't need to be a monster to do what Hitler did; you don't need some kind of supernatural powers. You just have to be in the right place at the right time. And you have to have a conscience. I'm sure he did. Or perhaps his madness just got in the way of everything else. Such a little man, who caused such suffering. No doubt it will happen again some day. People shouldn't look for monsters. They should worry about the ordinary man with too much ambition.'

Aside from the constant work, the other great hardship of Berlin life for Louise was the ever-present threat of bombing raids. The British were determined that an air campaign held the key to their success. In 1943, 207,000 tons of bombs were dropped on Germany. By 1944, that number had quadrupled to a staggering 915,000 tons. Between 1930-1945 a total of 61 German cities with a combined population of 25 million people had been attacked from the air. It is estimated that 3.6 million German homes were destroyed (or around 20 per cent of the nation's housing stock) and over seven million people made homeless.[11]

'We need to make the enemy burn and bleed in every way,' Churchill had insisted in 1941, and the unprecedented Allied aerial bombardment put that sentiment into practice.

The bombing campaign was as indiscriminate as it was intense. Describing the horrors of a firestorm that was created after an air raid over Hamburg in 1943, the local police chief wrote:

People jumped into the canals and waterways and remained swimming or standing up to their necks for hours until the heat died down. Even these suffered burns to the head. The firestorm swept over the water with its showers of sparks so that even thick wooden posts burned down to the level of the water. Children were torn away from their parent's hands by the force of the hurricanes and whirled into the fire.[12]

A British officer involved in the Battle of Berlin campaign offers a pilot's perspective on the carnage.

It was a very cold, clear night, snow on the ground. And it looked like a Christmas card scene down below. I hadn't seen that before. You could see the houses and the factories and the buildings. We dropped our bombs and you could see the buildings going up, see the houses exploding, see the bombs going along the street, erupting and blackening the snow.

Usually the target was obscured and you didn't get a good view of it. But to watch those houses going and to realise these were your bombs ... It was very, very disturbing.

Berlin between 1943 and 1944 was one of the most dangerous places on earth. During the Battle of Berlin, 27 per cent of the city was destroyed and more than 10,000 citizens killed.[13]

'When I first arrived in Berlin on my way to Potsdam, the city was still very much intact and services operated relatively normally. When I went back there to work with Goering, however, a lot of damage had already been done. The air raid sirens went off every single day and night, often more than once. It was difficult and frustrating, but we had to deal with it,' Louise said.

Of the countless air raids she experienced, there are two that remain most firmly fixed in Louise's memory, albeit for very different reasons.

'One of the first things I did when I arrived in Berlin and finally had some time off was to go to the opera. I was very interested in music and loved opera. The Berlin opera company was still performing, the opera house was still open.

'The first time I went to see a performance — *Aïda*, I believe it was — the sirens went off in the middle of it. The building's cellar had been reinforced and we all ended up in there — the audience, the production people, the singers and musicians. It was quite strange, and to be honest, I can laugh about it now after all these years.

'Here we all were, the audience nicely dressed, the musicians in their tuxedos and the performers in full costume and make-up, all sitting in this dark cellar waiting for the bombs to drop. I sat near the lead tenor. He was nervous; we all were.

'Later, when the all clear signal was given, everyone went back to their seats and the performers went back on stage. The performance carried on as if nothing had happened. It was a good performance too, if I remember. I know a story like that seems so bizarre now, almost like a joke, but that was how strange our lives had become; that was what war did to us all. We put up with a lot and always just tried to get through it in one piece.'

But there was nothing remotely funny about another air raid that hit several months after the opera incident.

While she had been given no clear indication of how long her services would be required in Berlin, Louise had assumed she would be gone from Potsdam a week or two at the most. After four weeks had passed in the Goering HQ, Louise found herself desperately short of clothing, having brought only a small bag with her from Supreme Command. One free evening, she caught the fast train back to Potsdam, collected more clothing from her hotel room, and then headed straight back to Berlin that same evening.

'The train pulled into Berlin and I had just climbed off, suitcase in hand, when the sirens started. There was panic of course, but at the same time, people were used to this happening. There was a very large shelter near the railway station, underneath a six-storey building. I ran to that.

'Soon there were about 100 people in that shelter, even some dogs that howled constantly at the sirens. At first, I hoped that this raid would be like all the others — some were false alarms, other times the bombs fell in another part of the city. This time was different, however.

'A bomb dropped directly on the building above us. It collapsed into a pile of rubble. Thankfully, the shelter withstood the impact and we were all unharmed. However, the debris from the building had trapped us inside, and it took a couple of hours for the air raid wardens to dig us out.

'It was terrifying, of course, and I was very relieved once they managed to partially open the shelter door. I ended up crawling out on my hands and knees over bricks and broken glass, still dragging my little suitcase behind.'

Once back out into the open air, Louise was confronted by a hellish scene.

'Everything was on fire. There was rubble all around, and everything that could burn was alight. People were running everywhere; it was very confused. The heat from the flames was so intense that it had melted a big area of tar on the road. People had become trapped in the melted road; it was as sticky as honey. These people were screaming in pain. The melted tar had caught fire in some parts as well. The people trapped were being burnt alive. I'd been running, but I remember I stopped when I saw those people on fire. I wanted to help them, but there was nothing I could do. Some soldiers appeared and they were yelling directions at the crowd, telling them which way to go to safety. Then I heard gunshots and I realised the soldiers were shooting the people who were burning, putting them out of their misery.

'A soldier told me to run to a nearby park and pointed out the way. As I ran in that direction, some timber beams from a building fell right behind me. They were smouldering and when they fell, the sparks caught my skirt and set it alight. Luckily, some other people rolled me on the ground and put it out before it could do too much damage.

'We waited in the park until the raid was over and then I had to walk for an hour to get back to my office. It was early morning by now. It was a difficult walk, I was in pain from the burns on my backside and I was in shock, I suppose. My skirt was a burnt mess, but I didn't think to change it.

'When I finally made it back to the office, I was told off for being late. Then, when they saw what had happened to me, they relented a little, but there wasn't a lot of sympathy really. Everyone had seen this kind of thing before and at least I was still alive and relatively unhurt. I sat down at my desk straight away and started working. I waited until the next morning to have a doctor look at my burns; I didn't want to risk getting into more trouble by asking for a little time off that day. The only good thing to come out of it all was I managed to keep hold of my suitcase through it all.'

A month after Louise's lucky escape, Goering's usual secretary recovered from her illness and returned to work. Shortly afterwards, Louise found herself once more on the fast train back to Potsdam and her old job. There were no goodbyes from Goering and few regrets from his replacement secretary about leaving the German capital.

'There were certain things I would miss about Berlin, but I was just glad to get away from it, actually. I felt relieved I'd got out alive. Not that Potsdam was a much safer place now. A couple of weeks after I returned, they decided to move the girls out of our hotel and put us up permanently at the Supreme Command Headquarters. A week later, that hotel was bombed and not a single person staying there got out alive. Nowhere was safe.'

Fate had presented Louise Fox with a rare opportunity to closely observe one of history's most infamous players. What she saw was a man of considerable ability, of significant privilege, of abundant charm;

a man who could perhaps have achieved great things had he not been so determined to seek out power at any price.

'He was friendlier and more open than most of the high-ranking Nazis I met. And I do believe that friendliness was genuine mostly. I think Goering was a man who wanted to be liked. I don't think Hitler cared what people thought of him, as long as they did what they were told. But Goering, with his jokes and his fancy uniforms — to me that shows he was a man who enjoyed being admired.

'Had he not been under so much stress, he would have been a very good-natured man I think. As it was, he was the happiest boss I ever had. I liked him in that regard; he was an easy man to like. Perhaps that's partially why he had achieved so much in such a short space of time.

'But you must realise that at the time I didn't know about all the lies, about the terrible crimes the Nazis were committing. If I had known the full story of what was going on in and around Germany every day, I would have seen Goering in a very different light. He, on the other hand, knew exactly what was really happening — he knew that we were losing the war, he knew about the Jews and others being murdered. He may have seemed harmless enough, but underneath he was a very dangerous person.

'Perhaps in some ways he had no choice but to be ruthless. Once he had achieved his position and his power, the only way to keep it was to be assertive and to order others to do things he himself perhaps didn't really agree with. But I don't want to make excuses for him. He deserved what he got in the end. All the Nazi high command did.

'Hitler, Goering, Goebbels — they were all power hungry, they would do and say anything to keep control of Germany. But I don't think Goering was mad, not in the same way that Hitler certainly was. Goering had just been corrupted by power and was prepared to sacrifice everything for it.'

There is one particular photograph and accompanying story of

Goering that is particularly memorable — amusing and strangely insightful at the same time.

It shows the Reich Marshall playing tennis in the opulent grounds of Carinhall in the latter years of the war. By this time, Goering's girth was at its most expansive; he wears immaculate tennis whites and oddly enough, a hairnet. His moon-face carries a definite look of annoyance and he appears to be glaring at the unseen player on the other side of the net. A guest at Carinhall would later recall that Goering had become furious when he was unable to return some impressive serves from his opponent.

'Can't you see where I'm standing?' he had demanded, seemingly unaware both of the actual point of tennis and the comical effect of his outburst.[14]

Louise laughed heartily and knowingly at the anecdote.

'I haven't heard that story before,' she said. 'But it certainly sounds like it could be true. It sounds exactly like the Goering I knew.'

5 A TERRIBLE DEFEAT

Reality is not protected or defended by laws,
proclamations, ukases, cannons and armadas.
Reality is that which is sprouting all the time
out of death and disintegration.
Henry Miller

BACK IN POTSDAM, it was General Langemeier's birthday and his staff decided to celebrate with a party. Despite an overwhelming workload, parties both spontaneous and planned were not unheard of at Luftwaffe Supreme Command.

'We grabbed our fun with both hands wherever we could,' Louise told me. 'We had to make the most of our time because we could all have been dead the next day.'

General Langemeier's party, however, would leave a lasting memory.

'Someone suggested we make a punch and we all thought that would be good idea. But when we worked out how many people would be there, we were worried we had nothing large enough to hold that much liquid. Then, we thought of a bathtub. It was perfect.

'Myself and some other girls went out into the forest and picked as many strawberries as we could find. Next, we filled a bathtub with ten bottles of wine, ten bottles of champagne, ten bottles of whatever we could find, and so on. It was a lot of fun, a lot of excitement for us. We were laughing and giggling, running madly about in search of bottles. When he had enough alcohol, we put the strawberries and sugar in and left it overnight.

'Unfortunately for our punch, there was a young officer stationed temporarily at our headquarters. He had been wounded in battle and was recovering on light duties. The same day we made our birthday punch, this officer decided to take a bath. When he discovered the punch, he obviously decided his bath was more important. Without saying a word to anyone, he pulled the plug and watched the whole lot go down the drain.

'Why he didn't ask someone about it, or just find somewhere else to take a bath, is beyond me. Arrogance I suppose. Or perhaps he didn't like punch!

'At first I was very annoyed when I found out what had happened. And I think some of us were worried that General Langemeier would be annoyed at the waste and also at the lack of punch on his birthday. But then when General Langemeier found out, he couldn't stop laughing. He was a man with quite a good sense of humour, luckily for us. After that, we were all able to see the funny side of it.'

By the last weeks of 1943, wasted tubs of champagne and other follies were still something to smile about at Supreme Headquarters — a situation unimaginable to millions of ordinary Germans forced to survive on ever-dwindling rations.

Despite the obvious privileges of their position, Louise said she and her fellow workers felt no guilt at their giddy excesses.

'No, no guilt whatsoever. We had to work hard, harder than just about everyone else in the country. We believed we were entitled to something extra; that the food and drink were an entitlement for the long hours we put into the war effort. It wasn't as if we were having large parties every day. There was still plenty of work to be done. But, yes, we enjoyed ourselves. There was always a little party going on somewhere, usually at night. That was when we drank our champagne mostly.

'We had an officer there who owned a large estate in the country.

Sometimes he would send men to his estate and have them bring back fresh vegetables, fruit, some meat perhaps. Even fresh cream for our strawberries.

'It is easy in hindsight to think we should have given more thought to other people. But the reality was we had access to these goods and others didn't. If I didn't drink the champagne, who would it benefit? Just someone else in the Potsdam headquarters. Of course we knew that thousands of our men were dying every day in battle, and thousands of our citizens were being killed in bombing raids. But what could we do about it? Everyone in those headquarters was working as hard as they could and putting as much effort as humanly possible into helping Germany win the war. I have no doubt of that.

'When people are stressed and fearful for their lives — and we all were at least some of the time — they have an instinct to look after themselves first and foremost before others. It is the instinct of self-preservation. Every living creature has it. Man is no different. We were no different. Guilt was a waste of time. We took what little pleasure we could and simply enjoyed it without thinking too much about the consequences. Grab the good times, we used to say, because the bad times will come of their own accord. And of course, they did.'

In fact, 1944 dawned with nothing but bad times for the German war effort. By January, Soviet troops were making significant headway into Poland and the Polish resistance was becoming increasingly effective. By March, the Allies were feeling bold enough to begin a series of long daylight bombing raids on Berlin, which until then had been largely targeted under the cover of darkness. On 5 June, the Allied forces entered Rome, ending the fascist dictatorship of Benito Mussolini. The following year he would be finally captured by Italian partisans, and tour his homeland for the very last time — his body tied to a truck and bouncing unceremoniously along cobblestone streets, much to the delight of the local populace.

The day after the Allies reclaimed the Italian capital, some 160,000 Allied troops under the command of General Dwight Eisenhower landed at five beaches along the northwest coast of France. Codenamed Operation Overlord, but better known as the Normandy landings, the campaign aimed to liberate France from German control. Despite meeting heavy resistance, the Allied troops were able to gain valuable ground inland and secure safe landing zones for reinforcements. Nine thousand German troops are estimated to have perished trying to defend the French coastline, along with some 6000 Allied soldiers. The German stranglehold over France was being slowly prised open, one desperate and bloody finger at a time.

Four days later, on 10 June, the panic which must inevitably have been rising in French-based German divisions was given a horrific voice. The little French village of Oradour-sur-Glane was picturesque and charmingly provincial. Its small population had been significantly reduced by the war, and those villagers that remained were mostly women and children or men too old or infirm to offer much resistance. The SS Division that entered the town that day ordered the entire population — some 652 people — to assemble in the town square. They then separated the men from the women and children, after first 'liberating' the locals of any valuables during a house-to-house search for weapons. The women and children were taken to the local church and locked inside. The assembled men were simply shot where they stood. The church was then burnt down, with no one able to escape through the heavily barricaded doors. A priest who visited the village the following day reported finding the charred bodies of 15 children huddled together and helplessly seeking sanctuary behind the still smouldering church altar. Only 10 people were known to have survived the massacre, which ranks as one of the worst wartime atrocities committed on French soil. Oradour-sur-Glane has never been rebuilt and today is a monument to German atrocities.[1]

The next month, more Nazi atrocities would come to light when the Red Army liberated the first concentration camp in Poland, at Majdanek.

On 20 August 1944, liberation of another kind took place when the Allies entered Paris to a triumphant reception. The liberation of the French capital sent an unequivocal signal to the Nazis that France had fallen from their grasp. Verdun, Dieppe, Artois, Rouen, Antwerp and Brussels all fell like dominos within a month, while Athens came under Allied control on 11 October. By mid-December, the fiercest fighting had moved to the Ardennes on the German/Belgian border. Fought in the bitter cold, the Battle of the Bulge represented Germany's final stand, a last defiant shake of the fist at the enemy. It was the largest land battle of modern history. More than one million soldiers took part and casualty rates on both sides were tragically high. When, after weeks of intensive fighting, it became clear that the Germans were losing ground, Hitler opted for a strategy he described as the 'Great Blow'. Against strong advice from Luftwaffe command and military specialists, he ordered squadrons of Luftwaffe planes to bomb Allied airfields in Holland, Belgium and France. The plan was to destroy Allied air power, but the strategy was foolishly risky and given the far superior strength of Allied ground artillery, doomed to failure. The Luftwaffe was decimated, losing more than 300 planes and 280 trained pilots in a little over two hours. Germany retreated on 8 January and the fall of the Third Reich was now a fait accompli.

For those working in Potsdam, the very real likelihood that the Fatherland would lose yet another war was beginning to make an impact on staff morale.

'By early 1944, conditions in Potsdam had changed. Things were definitely gloomier. There was a sad mood around the place. People didn't laugh so much any more. Oh, the work stayed the same of course. We were all still expected to work until we dropped if necessary, but the drinking and the gourmet foods had been slowly reduced. I don't think it was because the war was going badly; more likely because our generals simply couldn't get as much booty as before.

'The other thing that had changed too was the attitude of the staff. Before, we hadn't been allowed to talk about how the war was progressing, but I think we all had hoped that it would be over quickly and that, of course, we would be victorious. By 1944, everyone knew the truth. We still didn't speak about it openly, but we all knew the situation was hopeless. I was still working in ammunition supply, and I was having increasing problems finding ammunition to send out. My job was basically like that of an accountant except, instead of money, I was dealing with guns. I would consult supply lists and then check them against request documents. It was a matter of weighing up supply against demand. As the war progressed, that became an increasingly difficult job. By 1944, it was simply an impossible job. We were taking losses on too many fronts, and our factories could not supply new weapons quickly enough. Raw materials were also a problem — we were simply running out of materials, manpower and even the manufacturing facilities themselves due to enemy bombing campaigns.

'Later on, after the war was lost, it would become clear that Germany was simply not ready to fight. We would all come to realise that Hitler had made a terrible, stupid mistake by starting the war before we were properly prepared. Perhaps he was badly advised by his generals — dictators often get lied to by their advisers because everybody is too frightened to give them bad news. Or perhaps Hitler really didn't believe Britain would join the war. Who knows? But in 1944, sitting at my desk in Potsdam, I didn't know anything about how badly prepared we had been from the start. All I knew was that our soldiers were not getting the guns and bullets, or often even the food and medicine, that they needed.

'At my level of seniority, I wasn't in a position to determine what weapons went where. I was very pleased about that. All I could do was report on what was available and what was needed. My superiors were the ones who made those kinds of decisions. By 1944, that sort of responsibility must have been a terrible burden really. The situation had become desperate for our soldiers just about everywhere — a decision not to meet a request for new rifles and more ammunition could often have cost the lives of hundreds of men. Naturally, our commanders never said anything publicly to us about the situation. Behind closed doors, in their own private meetings, I'm sure they said a lot. We just kept on working and never asked too many questions. It wasn't our place and we knew it.'

Whether the civilian population had also lost faith in victory is less clear. The long hours and relative isolation of Potsdam meant that Louise had largely lost touch with life outside the Luftwaffe machine.

'I'm sure the public was still being fed Goebbels' lies. He would have been giving speeches on the radio, and writing long articles for the newspapers. As I have said before, in many ways he had a higher profile than Hitler himself. He was in the media more and he expressed his views on just about everything, from education to social issues like marriage and children. He wanted to give the impression he was like a father to the German people, watching over us. That was the excuse given for so many policies introduced by the Nazis — they would insist they were doing only what was necessary to help restore Germany to greatness. If people were put into prison, it was not because they were political enemies, but because they were enemies of every German. Joining the Nazi Party was compulsory for many citizens, not because Hitler needed obedience but because it was a way of showing your loyalty to the only group capable of helping our country. That was the tactic Goebbels used. True, Hitler was obviously in charge, but he tended to only take the spotlight on big occasions. So, even though I had little time to read newspapers or listen to the radio, I'm sure the propaganda would have been still going strong. The lies would have been as big as ever, too. Victory is just around the corner, and so on. Whether people still believed it or not, though, I can't say. I find it hard to believe that most wouldn't have started to doubt what the government was saying by this time. Conditions were so hard and dangerous for most in Germany — they would have been fools to believe we were headed for victory.'

Louise greeted the growing certainty her country was heading towards inevitable defeat with a curious mixture of despair and relief.

'Naturally, I was very saddened when it became clear we had little chance of winning. I had worked so long and hard, I had poured my heart into my work believing that if everyone did the same, we could win the war. It is true that I had never felt any great passion for either the Nazi cause or the reasons Hitler gave us for starting the war in the first place. But — and you must remember I was only a young girl at the time with little interest in politics or world affairs — once it had become clear that war was on the agenda, I was patriotic enough to support it and hope for our victory. The knowledge that we were going to lose was in some ways a heavy burden and a major disappointment.

'However, in some ways, there was a part of us that was glad. At least our defeat would mean an end to the fighting. And an end to the bombing and the rationing and the fear. I would much rather we had won, that's obvious, but I was so tired of the way we were living our lives that any conclusion seemed preferable to none at all. I guess I saw it as just wanting something — anything — to happen.'

In March of that year something did happen to, at least momentarily, break the grim monotony of life in Potsdam HQ. Following orders from Goering, Louise's entire department — several hundred staff — were instructed to move to a new base in East Prussia. The journey — which took over a week on a private Luftwaffe train — was designed to ensure that key Luftwaffe staff would be able to monitor more closely the activities and progress of the Red Army along the Eastern Front.

As she soon discovered, champagne and strawberries were not a priority at the new East Prussian base.

'The East Prussian HQ was quite different to ours. For a start, it was full of typical Prussian soldiers — all very straight and stiff upper-lipped, as the English would say. They were very professional, very orderly. But they would have been horrified at some of the fun we used to get up to in Potsdam. No punch in the bathtub or merry birthday parties for them. Everyone sensed this different atmosphere right away, and we just went along with it. We were guests really and to be truthful, I think by this stage most of us were too weary of the war and working to care too much about parties and cognac any longer.

'The East Prussian base was also very close to the Red Army, so it was in a far more vunerable position than Potsdam. If the Russians started to head our way, the base could be invaded within a couple of marching days. Being that close to the enemy — especially the Russians who were very much feared by most of us — tended to make things a little more serious.'

There was still time for some light-hearted diversions, however. As an incentive for their efforts, staff were occasionally offered the chance to take a field trip to see Hermann Goering's private villa, located in a forest near the town of Goldap.

'We hopped on a bus, all quite excited. The countryside was very beautiful: huge lakes, woods that were so wild they still had wolves living in them. It was snowing a little that day I remember; it was cold but clear. A lovely day and the snow looked beautiful on the trees. Goering's house was made out of wood — like a traditional German holiday house, only much, much larger. It was incredible to see. Surrounded by the forest, it looked very beautiful, almost like a picture-book house. Inside, I had never seen such luxury before. We were given a tour of the house and offered some drinks. I saw fabulous silk wall hangings, solid gold taps and carpet so thick that it touched your ankles as you walked. And remember, this was only one of his holiday homes! He had several houses — including some castles — in different parts of the country. There were two stuffed wolves at the entrance — Goering had killed them himself. He was a keen hunter, you know; it was his favourite pastime.

'Another thing that struck me about the house — apart from its incredible size and expensive furnishings — were the paintings hanging on the walls. They were everywhere, so many. The soldier in charge of our guided tour told us Goering had chosen them himself and that they had come from all over Europe, including the Louvre. Of course, what he meant was that they were stolen. God knows what they were worth.

'What I remember most though were the chairs. Goering was a very fat man and he had his chairs specially made so he could fit into them. They were huge. Three girls got into just one chair and they fitted in easily. We were all laughing at that. Of course, Goering himself wasn't home that day, otherwise we would never have dared.

'Looking back, I suppose you could describe the house as kitsch. It was opulent and built of the finest materials available, but the whole thing was done in a very heavy-handed manner. It was as if Goering was trying to brag about how much he had. There was nothing restrained about Goering, I suppose, so it was not surprising his house was over the top.

'A few months later, I heard that the Red Army finally reached the house. I imagine the staff were long gone by this stage, but I doubt very much that the paintings and furnishings would have all been removed to safety. There were simply too many. The Russians, knowing who the house belonged to, poured petrol all over the outside and set it alight. I'm sure they looted it first though. I often wonder about some of those priceless oil paintings — whether they were burned by some ignorant Russian who didn't know what they were, or whether perhaps they are still hanging somewhere in Moscow, even today. Such a waste.'

But by the time Goering's dream home burst into flames, Louise herself had left East Prussia, forced to evacuate by the continued advance of the Russians. Fearful of losing valuable staff, Luftwaffe Command ordered Louise's division to leave the area immediately and return to the slightly safer environs of Potsdam.

'When we got word that we were returning to Potsdam, I was quite pleased. Apart form the visit to Goering's house, I hadn't really enjoyed my time in East Prussia very much. The countryside was very beautiful of course, but we hardly ever got the opportunity to explore it. It was not a pleasant feeling knowing that the Russians were so near, either. Potsdam seemed a much better place to be. On 20 July 1944 — I remember clearly because it was the day before my birthday — we boarded our train to head back.'

However, it wasn't long before Louise realised that the meaning of 'safe' had become very relative indeed.

'The trip back from East Prussia took several days, and they were uneventful. Before arriving at Potsdam, the train had to stop at Berlin. We were just pulling into the station when, suddenly, the air raid sirens went off and a bomb fell very close to the railway line. The train wobbled madly from side to side, but thank God it wasn't a direct hit. In an instant, we were all lying face down on the floor, hands covering our heads. There was silence in the carriage for a minute as everyone waited to see whether more bombs would drop. When it became clear the raid was over for the time being, I put my head up and shouted out to the others in my carriage: "Looks like we are back home again". That gave everyone a good laugh at least.'

In January 1945, Louise's department received another order to evacuate — this time from Potsdam HQ. It would be the last mobilisation the group would ever be called on to make.

'The situation in the area around Berlin was unravelling quickly. It was crazy. East Prussia was of course lost to us by then and the Russians were moving towards the capital at great speed. They were like machines, those Russians — so tough and uncompromising. The speed at which they advanced on Berlin surprised many people on our side I think. We tended to view the Russians as unsophisticated and brutish; we didn't regard them as soldiers in the same way we did the British, or even the Americans to a lesser degree. We didn't have much respect for the Russians, at all. So perhaps we underestimated them. They could certainly march.'

By now, both Berlin and the city of Potsdam itself were virtually shut down. All those able to flee had already done so or were making frantic preparations to leave. In truth though, for the vast majority of people, there was simply nowhere to run.

'Where could people go? The enemy — the Russians, the British, the Americans — were marching all over the country. There weren't really many places left to hide. And most people simply didn't have the resources to run. Food was scarce, fuel was virtually impossible to get for a civilian. Both Potsdam and Berlin started to look like ghost towns. Windows were boarded up, curtains drawn, every shop and official building closed. The streets were usually empty — those people who had to go out tended to hurry back inside as soon as they could. I think most people had little choice but to lock their doors, bolt their windows and pray that the Russians would leave them unharmed. It was a terrifying time. We were in danger too, of course, but we were lucky in many ways. We were given the opportunity to escape.'

Immersed in the secluded cocoon of Supreme Command, Louise and her peers had been spared much of the deprivation and suffering inflicted on their countrymen by the demands of war.

'We knew about ammunition and weapon shortages, about supply and inventory. We knew things were bad, but at least we had food, we had shelter and though we certainly weren't safe, we had better facilities than lots of other people. In some ways we were sheltered from the worst of it.'

When it became clear that Berlin was lost, Louise's department were told to head south, to the mountainous region around Berchtesgaden, near where Hitler had his country headquarters.

The train trip south soon offered Louise a startling insight into just how desperate Germany's position had become.

'Our train was delayed at Jena, about one third of the way to Berchtesgaden. The line had been bombed further up, and we were stranded until it could be repaired. We just stayed on the train — not very comfortable I suppose, but we were far better off than those we had left behind. On the second day, a battalion of our infantry soldiers approached us. They asked if we had pushbikes on board. We said yes, of course. I had brought my own bike; I liked to ride it whenever I had some free time. What those soldiers did next amazed me. They yelled at us and told us they were confiscating our bikes. They took every pushbike off that train and then rode off on them. The reason? They had no trucks, no cars and no vehicles of any kind left. They were German soldiers on bicycles. That was what Germany had sunk to. We were fighting the Allies on pushbikes. It would have been funny if it wasn't so sad.'

A few weeks later, on 14 February, combined British and US forces began dropping bombs on Dresden, the capital city of Saxony and a major meeting point for German refugees from the east. The bombing of Dresden would prove to be one of the most controversial Allied campaigns of the war, and is widely regarded as a war crime by objective definition. Over a 48-hour period — and in spite of the city having no significant military installations — over 500 heavy bombers flew over the city, releasing so-called firestorm bombs — incendiary devices filled with highly combustible chemicals.

Lothar Metzer, whose infant twin sisters were killed in the bombing, was nine years old when his home town became a fireball.

We saw terrible things; cremated adults shrunk to the size of small children, pieces of arms and legs, dead people, whole families burnt to death, burning people running to and fro ... Fire everywhere and all the time the hot wind of the firestorm threw people back into the burning houses they were trying to escape from ...[2]

The Dresden dead numbered more than 135,000 and the city, long regarded as one of the most beautiful in Europe, was utterly decimated.

In Berchtesgaden, news of the Dresden raid was scarce and Louise cannot recall even being aware of what had taken place there until after the war.

'But it is the truth that German people suffered very badly. Sometimes I think that is forgotten because we lost the war and history is written by the winners. In Dresden, in Berlin, in many parts of Germany, people were bombed and killed in their millions.'

Berchtesgaden itself was a surreal place. Favoured by Hitler for its alpine splendour, fresh air and close proximity to his native Austria, the area had developed into a type of Nazi nirvana and de facto second seat of government — a staggeringly beautiful retreat in the mountains where Hitler's favoured acolytes would gather to meet, party and plan. Goering had a vast villa near Hitler's own home, Albert Speer had an architectural workshop, while Martin Bormann ran an experimental farm nearby. Hitler's Eagle's Nest Lodge, perched atop the Kehlstein Mountain more than a mile above sea level and with wondrous views to Austria, is today a popular tourist attraction. Accessible by a 124-metre stone tunnel cut into the side of the mountain, Hitler's private hideaway was reached by means of an enormous elevator which took passengers from ground to mountain top in 40 seconds.

By now the German capital Berlin was a fairly surreal place as well, but for altogether more terrifying reasons. By early April, Russian troops had not yet broken through Berlin's ailing defences, but their artillery barrages along with constant Allied aerial bombardments had reduced the German capital to chaos and rubble. The populace was starving, terrified and desperate for an end to the fighting. In his 30-room bunker, 50 feet below the Chancellery building, Hitler raged and cursed his enemies and the failure of his vision, but rejected any suggestion of surrender. Goebbels issued ever more deluded radio pronouncements inventing hope and salvation where none existed. For once, even the master of manipulation failed to believe his own lies. He requested eight cyanide pills — one for himself, his wife Magda and each of their six children who had joined him in the bunker. Outside, the remnants of the Nazi SS roamed the streets. Largely leaderless and bereft of clear orders, they reverted to doing the one thing they excelled at — killing.

There were few men of fighting age left in the capital and even fewer who were willing to face the suicidal task of confronting the approaching Red Army. Many soldiers had in fact already deserted, donning civilian clothes and hiding in the homes of friends or family. The SS were determined that these men be found and punished. They also sought to swell the depleted German ranks by forcing young boys — many as young as 14 — to pick up a rifle and defend the city. Those who refused or attempted to escape received a brutal lesson in SS justice.

Dorothea von Schwanenfluegel was a 29-year-old Berlin housewife who survived the fall of the city by huddling in her apartment together with her child and various neighbours. Her recollections of a city in its death throes — and the brutal anarchy that arose amidst the desperation — are graphic and compelling.

When trees were not available, people were strung up on lampposts. They were hanging everywhere, military and civilians, men and women, ordinary citizens who had been executed by a small group of fanatics. It appeared that the Nazis did not want the people to survive because a lost war, by their reckoning, was obviously the fault of us all. We had not sacrificed enough and therefore we had to forfeit our right to live.

Dorothea recalls walking along a near deserted city street one day in early April 1945 and hearing sobs coming from nearby. In a bomb crater by the roadside she discovered a small, very malnourished boy cowering under a pile of rags. He was wearing an SS uniform several sizes too large and had an anti-tank grenade by his side.

> I very softly asked him what he was doing there. He told me he had been ordered to lie in wait here and when a Soviet tank approached he was to run under it and explode the grenade.
>
> I asked him how that would work but he didn't know. If I encouraged him to run away, he would be caught and hung by the SS, and if I gave him refuge in my home, everyone in the house would be shot by the SS.
>
> When I looked for him early next morning he was gone and so was the grenade. Hopefully, his mother found him and would keep him in hiding during those last days of a lost war.[3]

In the Luftwaffe's Berchtesgaden headquarters a strange calm had descended

'After all those years of frantic work, suddenly there was very little to do any more. Our supplies were so limited, and communications were very poor. Our generals weren't receiving regular orders any more and they didn't know what to order us to do. And so we basically just sat and waited. Some people chatted, others took the opportunity to catch up on sleep. Others wrote letters to their families — although there was no way of posting them any more. It was the type of situation where some people handled it better than others. I never saw anyone panic though, which is probably surprising. Perhaps we were all too well trained, or perhaps the whole situation just seemed so unreal that people were having a difficult time accepting it as reality. Our officers tried to keep our morale up, but nobody made any speeches about the greatness of Hitler or how we could still defeat our enemies. Mostly they were quite kind to us, a little less stern than they had been in the past. To some extent we were all returned to being human beings again, rather than military people. There was still a chain of command, a definite structure. But everyone seemed to soften, even the officers. It was as though even the prospect of the war ending had started to change everyone.'

It was during this hiatus that Louise received her cyanide pill.

'It was nothing much to look at. Just a small, white pill. Like an aspirin. They were handed out to everyone. Just one — I guess like everything else, supplies were low. They also gave every one of us a rucksack, some cooking implements that could be carried in the rucksack and a knife that had a lot of little tools that could be useful outdoors. Obviously, our commanders were anticipating that we might have to survive outdoors for a while. When they gave us the cyanide pill we were told that we had the choice whether to use it or not. It was made clear to us that we were not being ordered to swallow the pill when we were captured. It was our choice. It was the air force's way of doing us a favour, I suppose.

'A lot has been said about how cold and fanatical the German soldiers were. How they were brainwashed by the Nazis. And, at the higher levels of both the military and the government, that might have been true. But the average citizen like me — we were not fanatics. We didn't want to die. Our officers had no intention of asking us to kill ourselves before the enemy arrived. I suppose they could have. Whether many people would have obeyed is a different matter. Everyone was wanting to wait and see what would happen when the foreign troops came. We were just people too — with families and dreams and lives we wanted to get back too. We were no different from the Russians or the English. People often forget that.'

Not surprisingly, the distribution of cyanide did little to alleviate the gloom that had descended over the division.

'It was an uncomfortable feeling, having the pill there. I suppose it was a comfort in one way — it offered a far quicker death than rape and torture at the hands of the Russians. But that pill also meant that we had reached a do or die situation. Our lives hung in the balance. Some people made some feeble jokes about it, trying to lighten the mood. But I don't think it really helped all that much.'

Despite her fear, Louise had no doubt that she would have opted for suicide had the need arisen.

'Oh yes, I was quite prepared to use it. No doubt about that at all. For most of us, the decision was that if we were captured by the Russians, we would use the pill. If the Americans got us first, then we would not. The Russians had an awful reputation; they were believed to be very barbaric, raping women, killing children. They destroyed and killed for the sake of it. Nobody wanted to fall into their hands. Later, when the Russians took over East Germany, 16 million people tried to flee from them. The stories of what they did to people are terrible. They took pregnant women and cut their bellies open with bayonets. That is a fact. That was not a fate I was interested in. So you can see why I kept that pill, just in case.'

One man who wasn't waiting around was Goering. While Hitler and many of his key henchmen opted to tough it out by remaining in the Führerbunker, Goering's highly tuned sense of self-preservation saw him leave Berlin on 22 April, the day after the first Russian troops marched into the outskirts of Berlin.

Goering flew to his villa at Berchtesgaden, along with a gaggle of bunker staff that had been given the chance to leave the city by Hitler. On learning that Hitler was refusing to leave the bunker — and would therefore face inevitable death either at his own hands or those of the Russians — the former flying ace decided the time was right to remind Hitler of his promise that the German leadership should revert to Goering if circumstances made it necessary. Now, with Germany effectively cut in half — the

Russians in charge of Berlin and the north, the Americans marching through the south — there seemed no more appropriate time for Goering to pick up the reins.

Indeed, Hitler himself had formalised the arrangement in June 1941 by naming Goering as his successor in a widely publicised and legally binding decree.

A carefully worded telegram — which veered in tone between fawning and forceful — arrived at Hitler's hideout on 23 April.

My Führer

Since you are determined to remain in your post in fortress Berlin, do you agree that I, as your deputy in accordance with your decree of 29.6.41, assume immediately total leadership of the Reich with complete freedom of action at home and abroad?

If by 2200 hours no answer is forthcoming, I shall assume you have been deprived of your freedom of action. I will then consider the terms of your decree to have come into force and act accordingly for the good of the people and the Fatherland.

You must realise what I feel for you in these most difficult hours of my life and I am quite unable to find words to express it.

God bless you and grant that you may come here after all as soon as possible.

You most loyal Hermann Goering.[4]

Louise remains in no doubt that Goering was acting primarily in good faith and that he had every reason to legitimately claim leadership.

'Everyone knew that Goering had been chosen by Hitler to succeed him. It was something that had been publicised in the past. There would have been no reason for Goering to think that Hitler would change his mind.'

But Hitler had indeed had a change of heart. The Luftwaffe's failure had seen Hitler lose faith in his former golden boy, while Goering's long sojourns at Carinhall and his frequently cartoonish public behaviour had become a source of some embarrassment.

Hitler was outraged at Goering's telegram, and encouraged by Goebbels and Bormann — both fierce and jealous rivals for Hitler's favour — he accused Goering of high treason and demanded his arrest.

Before dawn on 25 April, Goering found himself locked in the palatial splendour of his own home. Far from being cowed, the Reich Marshall began to work his not inconsiderable charms on his SS guards, pointing out that Hitler was most probably already dead, that he was indeed now the legitimate leader of the Third Reich and that his continued imprisonment was illegal. Ultimately, it was probably the ferocity of the Allied air raids over Berchtesgaden that presented the most convincing argument. On 26 April Goering's villa took a direct hit from an RAF bomb and was completely destroyed. Goering, however, was no longer inside. He had persuaded his captors to travel with him to the slightly safer surrounds of his castle at Mauterndorf. He was now a prisoner in name only.

When news of Goering's flight reached Hitler, he ordered a search to be conducted of the general area in and around Berchtesgaden. In the early hours of 27 April, SS troops burst into Louise Fox's sleeping quarters at Luftwaffe headquarters in hot pursuit of Hermann Goering.

'I think it was about two in the morning. I hadn't been long asleep when suddenly the bedroom door burst open and in marched these soldiers. They were shouting, demanding to know where Goering was. I was tired and irritable. When they yelled at me to stand up I said to one soldier: "Do you think I have fat Goering hidden under my bed?" The next thing I know, I had a gun sticking into my ribs. The soldier said "Lady, you open your mouth again and I will shoot you." So, of course, I shut up.'

Goering in fact was then approaching his mountain-top eyrie where he would remain, protected by his former captors, until the Germans formally surrendered to the Allies.

In Berlin, Hitler's torrents of rage had been replaced with utter despair. As the Soviet bombardment reached frightening intensity — with even the vast Führerbunker sustaining limited damage — Hitler learnt that Heinrich Himmler, the man he had affectionately nicknamed 'der treue Heinrich' (faithful Heinrich), had sought negotiations with the Allies and even offered to surrender German armies in the west to Eisenhower.

He ordered that his former friend be found and arrested and had Himmler's chief representative, SS Lt. Gen. Hermann Fegelein, who was based in the Führerbunker, taken outside and shot immediately. How Hitler's mistress, Eva Braun, reacted to Fegelein's death is not known. The lieutenant-general was her brother-in-law.

Believing himself betrayed by both Goering and Himmler, and with the Soviets surely only days way from breaking down the Chancellery door, Hitler announced his intention to commit suicide. He dictated a last will and testament that named Grand Admiral Dönitz — until now a relatively minor player in Reich affairs — as his successor, and blamed the Jews for all his misfortunes. Intriguingly, it also carried what appears to have been a veiled reference to the gassing of the Jewish population.

> I further left no one in doubt that this time not only would
> millions of children of Europe's Aryan people die of hunger, not
> only would millions of grown men suffer death, and not only
> hundreds of thousands of women and children be burnt and
> bombed to death in the towns, without the real criminal having
> to atone for this guilt, even if by more humane means.[5]

He also announced his intention to marry his long-time mistress Eva Braun — a reward for her faithfulness and her decision to 'go to her death as my wife'. The wedding ceremony was held in the bunker's vast conference room, with Goebbels and Bormann serving as witnesses. There was champagne, sandwiches and gramophone music. Those present recall the new Mrs Eva Hitler being composed, gracious and to all appearances, genuinely happy.

At 2.30 pm the next day, with the Russians wreaking havoc just a block away from the Führerbunker, Hitler and his wife bade farewell to their remaining staff and entered Hitler's private quarters. Shortly thereafter, a single shot rang out. Otto Gunsche, Hitler's SS adjutant, was the first to view the bodies — Hitler with a self-inflicted gunshot wound to his right temple, Eva Braun dead on the floor from cyanide poisoning. The room smelt of gunpowder and bitter almonds. As Hitler had instructed, the bodies were later taken to the Chancellery courtyard and burnt, avoiding the possibility of their corpses being used as trophies by the Russians.

Shortly afterwards, German radio solemnly announced that Hitler had 'fallen at his command post in the Reich Chancellery, fighting to the last breath against Bolshevism and for Germany'.

Goebbels and his wife poisoned their six children on 1 May, and then were themselves shot in the back of the head by an SS man at their request. Their bodies were burnt too, but fuel was running short and both corpses were badly charred but far from destroyed. Goebbels' blackened body was in fact recovered by the Russians, who — no novices in the fine art of propaganda themselves — filmed and photographed the scene as testament to the complete capitulation of the fascist regime.

With Goebbels gone, the rush out the Führerbunker door commenced with rather unseemly haste. Everyone, including Martin Bormann, decided to take their chances in the outside world. Only a handful were able to escape the Russian troops, with Bormann making it only as far as the nearest railway station before being fired upon. His wounds were not fatal, but the cyanide capsule he took as he lay writhing on the ground most certainly was. His body was subsequently buried in rubble and lay undiscovered for decades. The lurid stories of

Bormann having escaped to Patagonia or Brazil or Paraguay were finally put to rest when his remains were discovered and formally identified in the late 1980s. Heinrich Himmler met a similar fate. He was captured by Allied forces attempting to cross the Swiss border. He had false papers and was wearing an eye patch in a rather feeble attempt at disguise. Despite being searched by British troops, Himmler still managed to avoid interrogation by swallowing a cyanide capsule secreted in one of his teeth, specifically hollowed out for the purpose.

On 8 May 1945, the entire staff of the Luftwaffe Supreme Command was formally dismissed from the air force. Germany's new Chancellor, General Dönitz, had made his only significant contribution as leader — the unconditional surrender of his armed forces to the Allies. It was a day that Germans would later come to refer to as Stunde Null — hour zero, the moment that the old regime ended and life began anew. They also heard for the first time the news of Hitler's death, as well as those of the Goebbels family. Suicide was not mentioned and few details were entered into. As usual, Louise and her colleagues asked no questions.

'The dismissal from the air force wasn't a shock. We'd all been expecting it for some time. There was no particular ceremony, nothing to really mark the occasion at all. Our commanding officer simply called us together and said we had been formally dismissed. They handed us papers which verified the fact. It was a grim moment, but in some sense we realised it could have been much worse. We were still alive, that was the most important thing. While there was life, there was hope. That is what I clung to and tried to draw strength from. I think the most common feeling in the room that day was a sense of gladness that the war was over. But what gnawed away at us now was the future. What would happen to us? That was what was so frightening. We'd escaped the bombing, but the area all around Berchtesgaden had been badly hit every day. Hitler's main villa, Goering's house, Bormann's farm — just about everything was gone. The Eagle's Nest survived of course, but I didn't know that at the time.'

Even Louise was surprised at her reaction on discovering the Führer was dead.

'I felt a sense of loss, really. I think most of us did. He had been our leader, he had given us direction, even if we didn't always like the way he took us. I had no love for Hitler, but he was the only real leader I had ever known and there was a feeling of slight shock that he suddenly wasn't there any more. I suppose at some level all those years of brainwashing had had an impact on me. I knew he was human — I'd seen him in the flesh several times — but accepting that he was dead was a little difficult.

'To be honest, I felt a little sad for him when I first heard the news. Things had got out of hand for him; he had created a situation which in the end he couldn't control. His downfall was that he wanted to start a war. If he had just gone on rebuilding Germany as he did in the beginning, he might have been a very good leader. But he wanted a war and he wanted money to pay for it. He took money from the Jews and from the government that didn't belong to him. We all suffered terribly because of his desire to wage war. But still, there was some disappointment that he was dead.

'Afterwards, I threw away the medal Goering had given to me. It had become a liability. Having such a thing in my possession would make me stand out from the others when we were captured. It made me look far more important than I was. Although I was quite proud of it, I had no problems throwing it away. I'd never really felt that I earned it anyway. It was just a medal — not worth possibly dying for, that's for sure. I kept the cyanide pill of course — hid it in the lining of my jacket — and even today I still have the document dismissing me from duty.'

Although by now they were aware that the Americans rather than the Russians would reach them first, it is perhaps odd that few in the Luftwaffe headquarters thought to run.

'Where would we go?' Louise responded. 'There was no transport, communications were down, and nothing was operating as normal. We just hoped that the Americans would treat us well if we co-operated. I was anxious, of course, about what might happen, but more than anything I was happy to see an end to the fighting. To be honest, one of my first thoughts when I found out the war was over was that, finally, I might be able to get some new clothes. Terrible, I know, but there comes a time when people just want things to return to normal, to get on with their lives. We were all so tired of war.'

Unlike the pathetic scenes inside the Führerbunker, senior Luftwaffe personnel remained in control of their emotions and few, if any, resorted to suicide.

'Nobody took the pills as far as I was aware. Of course, it was a big place, with hundreds of staff so I couldn't say that with certainty. For me, once I knew it was the Americans that would capture us, I had no intention of killing myself. And unlike Hitler and Goebbels, most of our officers were Prussian soldiers, well trained and dedicated. For them, suicide was beneath their dignity. It was a coward's way out. They had been taught that in surrender, a soldier must face the consequences as well as the enemy. They would have preferred to go to a prisoner of war camp and take their chances there.'

The arrival of American troops proved to be rather anti-climactic.

'They were mostly young and fairly polite, I suppose. I didn't think much of them really; they didn't impress me as much as I thought they might. I had never seen an American before, so I was scared but also curious. I remember some of the girls being more frightened of the black soldiers; we weren't used to seeing Negro people.'

The Luftwaffe staff were rounded up and marched to a nearby barracks previously occupied by German troops.

Shortly afterwards, a series of interrogations began for every prisoner, including Louise.

'They would come into the barracks with a sheet of paper and read off some names. If your name was on the list, you went with the soldiers. We were taken to a room on our own — usually it had nothing much but a couple of chairs and maybe a desk in it. Of course, the first time this happens, you are terrified. I had no idea what was going to happen to me. We had been told that the Americans would not rape or torture us — but of course, I couldn't be 100 per cent certain of that. I tried to look calm and collected — as though I wasn't frightened. I was too proud to give them the satisfaction of thinking they had scared me.

'As it turned out, the first American officer who interrogated me was probably more nervous than I was. He looked very young and unsure of himself. I don't think he knew what to do with me. He started asking me questions, quite politely really. They had seen my discharge papers and other identification. They knew I wasn't very high up in the air force ranks and that I wouldn't have had access to very much important military information. He asked me what I had done in my work, and I told him the truth. Once he realised I was going to co-operate, I could sense that he was relieved. Obviously, I was making his job easier for him. The only part of it that really interested the Americans was the codes that we used for sending secret information. I of course used that code every day, so I knew it very well. I told them all about the code, and they wrote down everything I said. That whole first session probably took only an hour or so. It wasn't pleasant; it was humiliating in many ways. Being a prisoner is degrading. But I soon figured out there was really nothing to be frightened of.

'There was never any violence involved in my interrogations. There was no threat of violence either, although of course, there was no need as I co-operated fully. I didn't hear of anyone else being beaten or killed, either.'

Louise is dismissive of what others might regard as her disloyalty to the German cause so soon after defeat.

'Why not? Why shouldn't I have told them everything? The war was over. It wasn't as though by refusing to speak, I was going to help the German cause. The only secrets of value I had were the codes, and the truth is that countless other prisoners in that camp knew exactly the same code. I'm sure most of them told the Americans too. None of us returned to the barracks after our interrogations and announced to everyone what we had told the Americans of course, but I'm sure the majority of people would have at least partially co-operated. It was something discussed quietly, between people that knew each other fairly well. Interestingly, there was never any pressure put on us from our peers to keep quiet either. We had all had enough by that time, I believe. Very few were interested in maintaining their hatred of the enemy or the pretence that we all wanted to go down fighting. We were tired. Most of my information was probably not very useful anyway. In fact, one American officer told me later on that they had used an almost identical code to our own.

'They simply asked me what I had done in terms of my work and I told them. I felt no need to be loyal and hold my tongue. What was the point?'

Conditions inside the converted barracks were spartan but otherwise agreeable.

'They fed us and the food was alright. We had a better chance of eating there than outside, that's for sure. It was basic army-style food. A lot of it was the type of dried and packaged rations that soldiers are given. But it was three meals a day, so we weren't complaining. Everyone had a camp-style bed with a blanket — they'd brought in extra beds to accommodate us all. The barracks were reasonably warm and there was a yard where we were allowed to wander around outside. I spent a lot of time out there when the weather was good, talking with people or just thinking about what the future might hold, not only for me, but Germany as a whole.

'The Americans were not too strict really — they kept an eye on us of course, but we were fairly free to chat and wander around during the day without too much interference.

'The most important rule that they maintained was the curfew at 8.00 pm each night — we weren't allowed to be seen outside our barracks after that time. They were very serious about that. We were warned about it repeatedly. And you had to be careful; the talk was that the Americans were fairly trigger-happy. Not so much because they were cruel, but because they were scared. Personally, I never saw anyone get shot, thank God, but there were plenty of gossips who claimed they had.'

For three weeks, Louise remained a prisoner of the Americans, being questioned on a regular basis, often being asked to repeat the same information over and over. At no time did the Americans give any indication of what her eventual fate might be at their hands.

'I didn't expect to be executed; I wasn't high ranking enough for that. But none of us knew that was going to happen next. When we weren't being questioned — and sometimes I might go several days without being called into the interview room — we basically had nothing to do but sit around and worry. It was very nerve-racking, very draining emotionally. We didn't know what was going to happen to us from one day to the next; we didn't know whether we would be sent to prison or whether we would be set free.'

Louise had also heard no news from her family for several months.

'I knew my father had been discharged from the air force because of his age. I knew he had been given additional duties before he was discharged. Instead of just playing in the air force orchestra, he was also assigned to the job of repairing communication lines, telephone lines. He was somewhere in the Balkans at that time. It was quite dangerous. They would have to climb up the telephone poles and try to make repairs. Of course, if an enemy plane was flying overhead they would try to shoot at them. I'd learnt from one of my father's letters that he and a colleague had been working on the same pole when his friend was shot and killed in front of him.

'Later, he was captured by the Russians and spent some time in a prisoner of war camp in Czechoslovakia. But he was lucky; although he had a terrible time there, the Russians eventually let him go. They thought he was too old to do them any harm. If he had been a young man he would have had a bullet in his head very quickly, no doubt at all.

'When I last had contact with my parents they had been transferred to Gdansk in Poland. My father had been put in the military reserves; he was now too old to fight in the normal army. They wrote and told me they were preparing to flee Gdansk, because the Russians were about to invade the city. My mother was to take the train, while my father would leave on a U-boat. My sister had been working at a factory in Vienna, but when it was blown up and completely destroyed she had to return to my parents in Gdansk. That was the last I had heard. The postal service stopped working at that point and wouldn't operate again for around seven months. So I had no way of knowing whether they were alive or dead. I wanted to see them again, to find out how they were. I wanted to get out of the camp too, I couldn't stand the waiting and uncertainty any more. That was when I decided to try to escape.'

In the 7th Army Interrogation centre in Augsburg, Louise's former Supreme Commander was finding the transition from leader to prisoner of war rather more difficult to adapt to.

Goering had surrendeed to American forces of his own volition in early May 1945. He had fully expected that he would be treated as the legitimate head of the German government and was therefore shocked to find himself eating soldier's rations, sleeping on a bunk bed and — most horrible of all — stripped of all his medals and insignia.

Even with his trappings removed, Goering remained as cunning and manipulative as ever.

Major Kubal, US camp commander at Augsburg, noted in a 19 May report:

He is by no means the comical figure he has been depicted as so many times ... He is neither stupid nor a fool in the

Shakespearean sense but generally cool and calculating. He is certainly not a man to be underrated. Goering is at all times an actor who does not disappoint his audience ...

The cause for which Goering stood is lost but the canny Hermann, even now, thinks only of what he can do to salve some of his personal fortune and to create an advantageous position for himself. He condemns the once-beloved Führer without hesitation. Up to now, he has not made a plea for any of his former henchmen, alive or dead.

Yet, behind his spirited and often witty conversation is a constant watchfulness for the opportunity to place himself in a favourable light.[6]

In the end however, even Goering could not charm his way out of the inevitable verdict at Nuremberg. Despite putting up a dogged and at times quite brilliant defence, Hermann Goering was found guilty of war crimes and crimes against humanity and was sentenced to be executed by hanging on 15 October 1946.

As in most things, Goering would only be accommodating as a means to an end. While prepared to offer both remorse and justification for his role in the Third Reich, Goering could ultimately not accept the fate his enemies had bestowed on him. So it was that just two hours before his execution was scheduled to be carried out, he was found dead of cyanide poisoning. Mystery still surrounds how one of the highest profile and most watched prisoners in world history was able to smuggle in and conceal a suicide pill and the finger of blame has subsequently been pointed at various figures, including his wife Emmy, thought to have passed it to her husband during their farewell kiss, and a prison guard who later claimed he had been bribed by an agent of the former Reich Marshall. The more likely theory is that Goering had probably had the pill for some months and may even have had it with him since the time of his surrender, cleverly secreted in the few possessions he was allowed to keep.

Goering's body was cremated in Munich and his ashes, together with those of nine other high-ranking Nazis also executed on the same day, were transported to a remote country road outside the city. There, in driving rain, the combined ashes were unceremoniously dumped in the mud.

News of his death had little impact on Louise.

'You know what I did when I heard? I shrugged my shoulders and said, so what? I had admired him, but by the time of his death, I was past admiring anyone. By then, every day was taken up with trying to find enough to eat just to stay alive. The country was in ruins. What did I care about Goering? I couldn't care less that he was dead. He meant nothing to me. His time was over. I had no sympathy left in me.'

6 THE AFTERMATH OF MADNESS

What difference does it make to the dead, the orphans and the homeless, whether the mad destruction is wrought under the name of totalitarianism or the holy name of liberty or democracy?

Mahatma Gandhi

IT WAS A TOSS OF A COIN that Louise was happy to lose.

After ten days of imprisonment by the Americans, Louise decided on a radical course of action, though it would take some time to work out how to implement it. Freed from the constraints of the military hierarchy, the defiant girl who hated doing as she was told was once again free to resurface.

'I couldn't spend another minute in that camp. I wanted to talk to my family, I wanted to get on with my life. More than anything, I wanted to go home. Back to Wismar, which had been the only home I had known before the war. I didn't know if my parents or my sister were even there any more, but it was the logical place to start looking. It was also somewhere familiar, and I think I really needed to return to something familiar after all that had happened over the last few years.

'For me, sitting and waiting and allowing the Americans to decide my fate simply wasn't an option any more. All through the war I had been under the command of others. My fate had never really been in my own hands. In fact, in some regards, the direction of my entire life up until then had been decided by others — my mother, my teachers, Adolf Hitler, the air force. With the war over and my old life so far away, I realised now — finally — I could take charge of my own destiny.'

While hardly salubrious, the accommodation offered in the makeshift prisoner of war camp was perhaps more comfortable than the living conditions being experienced at that time by the majority of Louise's countrymen.

'It was a typical sort of barracks really — big, long rooms with rows of metal beds. We were given a blanket, a pillow and some basic utensils like a plate and a spoon. The barracks were fairly crowded and noisy most of the time; there would have been hundreds of people imprisoned in them — but overall it wasn't too bad.'

The Americans had secured the perimeter of the barracks with barbed wire and it was overseen by regular patrols of armed soldiers. Despite these measures, Louise sensed that escape was a far from an impossible goal. Lack of preparation time and the overwhelming number of prisoners needing to be processed and accounted had led to a situation where camp security sometimes ran a poor second to the more pressing necessity of simply accommodating so many people.

'The Americans had very little time to get this camp ready. They had to take what they could get in terms of buildings — there was no time for them to build a new facility. The barracks were the best they could do. The problem for them was that the buildings were scattered over quite a large area — there were countless places people could hide. The sheer number of people they had rounded up — and the confusion that came with all of that — just made their task harder, I suppose. Some people had lost papers or were deliberately hiding identification — it must have been very difficult for them. Of course, most of us from the air force just co-operated. That was the profes-sional thing to do.'

The attitude of the Americans to their unaccustomed task as gaol keepers also created opportunities for prisoners to escape.

'The Americans were very casual I found — far too casual, really. That was a good thing for us as prisoners, of course. They were not particularly cruel or harsh people; they treated us generally quite well. But their soldiers were unimpressive, especially those in the lower ranks. They seemed to lack discipline, they did not seem very well trained compared to the German soldiers. They were, loud and arrogant, but not very observant. It didn't take me long to realise that with such guards, finding a way out of the camp would perhaps not be that difficult.'

It was a view that Louise soon discovered was shared by others.

'There were two other girls in the camp with me — Herga and Sabina. They were both from Nuremberg. They were around my age and both blondes, fairly typical looking German girls. I asked them one night if they wanted to escape and they said they did. Then we had to come up with a plan.'

There are few viable options open to young women who wish to impose their will on a battalion of gun-toting men. In the end, they had little choice but to draw on the most obvious weapon in their limited arsenal — their bodies.

'We tossed a coin to see who would go with one of the guards. We figured this was our best chance. We had no money or goods to bribe them with. And the fact that the Americans did not seem to us to be particularly good soldiers gave us plenty of hope our plan would work. How else could we have got out? Luckily for me, I didn't win the toss,' Louise said matter-of-factly.

But would she have carried on with the plan if the coin had dropped a different way and the task of entertaining a gullible soldier had fallen to her?

'Absolutely. It was something that had to be done. It wasn't pleasant but there were worse things. To us, this was not so important really. And you must remember that we didn't know what would happen to us if we stayed. We thought that if we could at least get out, we had a better chance. I have always said that extraordinary situations require extraordinary actions. And this was an extraordinary situation. You did things that you would never do in everyday life.'

Louise can no longer recall which girl fate singled out for the job but, regardless, the plan went even more smoothly than she had hoped.

'One of the girls found a soldier, flirted with him a bit and then, a few hours later, disappeared with him for a while. The next night there was a little hole cut in the wire fence on the perimeter of the camp, just as he had promised. I suppose it would have been simple for that soldier to have had his fun and then just not carry out his side of the deal. After all, it wasn't as if we could go and complain! Perhaps they didn't take us all that seriously, that was the impression I got anyway. They were only really interested in people much higher up the chain of command than us. We were small fry and of little consequence.'

Under cover of darkness the girls crawled through the opening, taking their Luftwaffe-issue camping gear with them. Surprisingly, the Americans had not attempted to confiscate most of the prisoner's personal possessions.

'They had taken away the knives the air force had given us as part of our outdoor equipment. The Americans said they were too big and they did not meet regulations. But I didn't hand mine in, I wore it hidden on a string under my clothes. As I said, there were just too many people and too much chaos for the Americans to have searched each one of us. In a more organised prisoner of war camp, I would never have got away with hiding something as lethal as a knife.'

Their jubilation at having made it outside the camp undetected was short-lived as the girls realised both the gravity of their situation and the fact that they had no clear idea of what to do next.

'We hadn't really thought it through, that is true. We only had a vague idea where we were going and how to get there. We had no food and only a few clothes and, of course, our rucksacks. We decided to keep wearing our uniforms because they were the warmest things we had, but we took off all the insignia. We'd thrown away our guns, of course; we'd got rid of them before the Americans even rounded us up. It would have been too dangerous to try to keep them once we were taken prisoner.

'The three of us spent the first night huddled under some bushes, terrified that they would send someone out to find us. It was May, summertime, but the nights could still get chilly. Still, once we had made the decision to leave, there was no going back. Of course, there were no trains running, very little transport of any kind apart from Allied vehicles. We had little choice but to start walking home.'

For Louise, home was a daunting 1000 kilometres away. The city of Nuremberg, home to her two companions, was about one third of the way to Wismar. It was decided to walk to Nuremberg first and then for Louise to continue on to the Baltic Coast alone. Taking back roads wherever possible and using the Rhine River as a navigational point, the girls' route took them through numerous small rural villages, which they initially assumed would have escaped much of the devastation. Within hours of starting their trek, however, they realised that there was virtually no corner of Germany that did not bear the scars of war in some way.

'I thought the villages would be intact, more or less. The Allies had begun by bombing the cities of course, but I suppose they ran out of cities. There was destruction everywhere. Roads were blown up, railway lines, even the houses of farmers. I don't know why they would even bother to destroy some of the things they did. I was stunned by what we saw; it was the first time I realised the full extent of the bombing.'

The need to eat meant that few villages could be bypassed. Avoiding people altogether, while reducing their risk of recapture, would have meant a slow and certain death through starvation.

'We had to beg for food from farmers. If they hadn't fed us, we would have died. Of course, we could have stolen, I suppose, but we didn't really need to. People did feed us, even though they sometimes had very little themselves. But they did usually have bread, potatoes and some other vegetables — that's what we survived on.'

They slept mostly in the open, some patch of bushy undergrowth on the roadside their only blanket. Occasionally, a farmer was willing to accommodate them in a barn where they nestled down happily with the livestock, delighted to be indoors if only for a few sleepy hours. Despite their status as escaped prisoners, few hesitated to help the girls if they were able.

'People did not fear retribution from the Allied soldiers at all,' Louise explained. 'The fact is that the rule of law had broken down. People did what they liked; it was every man for himself. Nobody really feared the American soldiers, except those who had been in the SS or were high-ranking Nazis. Everyone else was more concerned with finding food. The farming people were usually quite kind, and we met some nice people on the road. But underneath it all, we all knew that if we seemed to have more than someone else, they would probably find a way to take it. People wanted to survive. The only reason there wasn't a lot of theft and looting was because there was nothing left to steal. It would be nice to say everyone helped each other, but the reality was that didn't happen.'

The depths of Germany's lawlessness quickly became apparent when, after only a few days on the road, the girls came across a small settlement where they hoped to find something to eat. From a distance, it seemed a fairly typical village — a cluster of single-storey, rough-hewn houses gathered around a town square. As the girls drew closer to the centre of the village, however, it soon became clear that Allied bombs had not been the only threat confronting the local populace.

'There was a man hanging from a tree in the town square. Nobody had cut him down. We asked someone who he was and were told he had been the mayor. Apparently, when it became clear that the war was lost, he had hoisted a white flag in the centre of the village, hoping that when the enemy arrived they would not kill anyone else.

'Unfortunately for him, an SS squad came through first. They saw the flag and hanged the mayor for being a traitor. They were murderers really, most of them. He had just wanted to stop any more lives being lost, but the SS were fanatics, they couldn't accept that. The war was lost, but still they thought we should all die pointlessly anyway. Some villagers told us they had executed him the day before we surrendered. He died a day before the war finished. It was tragic and horrible to think that this was our own people that had done this.'

Louise would see five more corpses in five different towns before her journey ended.

'And I can tell you my dear, you never get used to seeing something like that,' she told me. 'Never.'

It took 17 days to reach the outskirts of Nuremberg.

'We had been walking around 20 kilometres a day — sometimes less. Our feet were very blistered and our backs ached from carrying the rucksacks, which were quite heavy. We were exhausted, I have never felt so tired. But, although they had reached home, I still had a long way to go.'

Louise did not take time to venture into Nuremberg itself for one simple reason.

'There was nothing left there any more. It was basically just rubble from what we could see. I didn't know anyone in the city, and I believed it would be harder to get food there than in the countryside where people weren't so dependent on rations. There wasn't anything for me in Nuremberg. So Sabina and Herga went together to look for their families. I was sad to see them go, of course, but we had always known we would separate once we reached their home city.'

She was never to see Sabina or Herga again, although they did correspond several times once the postal service began deliveries again.

'We did keep in touch, although not for very long really. We all had our lives to get back to. One of the girls — Sabina I think it was — managed to find her family still alive in the city. They even had somewhere to stay. Herga could not find her family at all, and her home was bombed out of existence. The last I heard from them, Herga was living with Sabina and her family. The poor girl had nowhere else to go.'

A constant stream of refugees both from within Germany itself, and foreign nationals of German heritage fleeing from violent anti-German sentiment in countries such as Poland and Czechoslovakia, ensured that even with her travelling companions gone, Louise never felt truly alone.

'The truth was there were people all over the countryside. Everyone was walking, either trying to get home or looking for a new home. Some people carried lots of possessions with them, others had nothing but the clothes on their backs. There was always someone to talk to if you felt like it.

'The people I met on my journey came from all over Germany and even from other countries. Everyone had a story to tell. I met soldiers who had walked from the Italian Alps where they had been fighting until the war was lost. They told me stories about men freezing to death in the snow, of men falling into mountain ravines, of being trapped under snowdrifts; starving and suffering horrible deaths.

'The most common story was that of people who had lost their homes or their families — and very often both. There were soldiers who had returned to their home town to find their house destroyed and all their relatives dead or missing. There were parents who had lost all their children, and children wandering together without parents. Nobody seemed to have any hope for the future; everything they knew had been taken away and they were still in shock really. People kept saying how they just couldn't believe what had happened, how everything had been destroyed. They were mostly glad to be alive of course, but there was so much sadness everywhere.'

Twice Louise was captured by American forces and questioned.

'I looked suspicious I suppose, walking around still in my uniform and on my own. On both occasions though, all they did was ask me a few questions — which I answered more or less truthfully, apart from the bit about escaping from the camp in Berchtesgaden, of course. They fed me, which was great because I was constantly hungry — and then let me go free both times after just a couple of days. They weren't interested in me, they were only after people who had been high-ranking, or who had been in the SS. There were too many people on the move for them to take much notice of someone like me.'

On one occasion she was locked in a cell with a group of men who she quickly discovered were former SS soldiers.

'I was a little shocked at first — after all, I had been scared of the SS for a long time, just like most Germans. In our minds they were a breed apart from the rest of us, some of them were no better than thugs and murderers. Hitler had taken some of them from gaol — he wanted violent men, you see. However, they were so pale and thin, they had haggard faces like old men, even though they weren't very old at all.

'When you see people like that, it changes your perspective. Suddenly, they were not just SS soldiers, they were human beings. I felt sorry for them, to tell the truth. They were suffering and no one deserves to suffer for long.'

Realising that Louise was not likely to stay in custody for long, three of the men asked an extraordinary favour of her.

'They asked if, once I got out, I could let their families know where I had seen them and that they were still alive. I agreed to do that. They all lived around the area where we were locked up. So it wasn't so difficult for me to do. Once I had agreed, they thanked me and then one said very quietly, "I don't think we will ever get out of here". Imagine thinking something like that. That you had no hope. Even when things were going so badly for me, I always had hope.'

On her release, and having memorised the names and addresses of the three families, Louise kept her promise. She located each family and passed on their messages, despite the task adding several days to her journey.

'The families were very grateful to me. Some of the wives cried — they were really concerned their husbands had been killed. It made me feel good to have done something, and I didn't mind the extra time it took. In truth, I had stopped trying to hurry. I still wanted to get home, but I had also begun to rediscover my sense of adventure. I was seeing parts of Germany I had never seen before — beautiful places despite everything. In a strange way, even this forced walk was not without its benefits. There was some good in it all.'

As for the SS men she left behind, Louise remains an optimist about their likely fate.

'Most of the SS men were put on trial by the Americans. And I think those trials were largely fair. Many got prison sentences, but some were excused and released back to their families. I like to think that those men made it home before too long.'

By week three of her trek, Louise's rucksack had become an almost unbearable burden to carry.

'I thought I would get used to carrying it around after a while, but I didn't really. It was never easy.'

Passing through some nameless town, she saw a child's billy-cart outside a house and realised in an instant that it was time to upgrade her mode of transportation.

'It was quite a large cart, the type with a handle that you can use to steer or to pull it along behind you. I stole that cart, I'm sorry to say. As I have said, on the road there weren't any laws, and after a while I guess that affected my thoughts too. I had that cart for the rest of my journey. I put my rucksack in it and pulled it along behind me on the cart — much easier than carrying it on my back. And when I came to the top of a hill, I would get in the cart along with the rucksack and race down. I probably looked like a madwoman, but I didn't care. It was better than walking. Of course, when I walked uphill, I had to drag the cart and rucksack with me, which wasn't so easy or nearly as much fun.'

Shortly after that, Louise reached the river Elbe, only to find that the bridge — the only way across the river on foot — had been completely annihilated by bombing. With her road to Wismar unexpectedly blocked, Louise sat down on a dyke and contemplated her next move.

'I was sitting there — feeling very disappointed and trying to think how I could get across this river some other way — when some other travellers came along. We started talking and they asked me where I was headed. I told them Wismar — that's if I could get across the water of course. That's when they warned me that the Russians had occupied Wismar and the towns around it. It's not safe, they said. You'd be mad to go there now. Right away I knew I had to change my plans. There was no way I wanted to go anywhere near the Russians. I just hoped at the time that my parents were away from the area too — that they hadn't tried to travel back to their home.'

With her plans in tatters and her destination seemingly as far away as ever, Louise had little choice but to make a detour.

'I sat on that dyke for quite a long time — thinking about what to do. Most of my relatives were in the north of Germany and that, of course, is where the Russians were. So I couldn't go there. Finally, I remembered that my father had a brother who lived in Cuxhaven, a port town that was also on the Elbe, at its mouth, where the river runs into the North Sea. It was in Saxony, and I had learned on the road that the area was controlled by the Americans and the English. That was certainly preferable to me.'

Rudolf Fox and his wife Elizabeth (invariably called Lizbeth by those who knew her well) had lived in Wismar during Louise's childhood. Rudolf was Fritz Fox's younger brother and, like his sibling, he was tall, thin, dark and quietly spoken. Their respective wives however, could not have been more different.

'My aunt Lizbeth was a simple woman really; she came from a rural part of Mecklenburg and probably wasn't a great conversationalist. She wasn't as clever as my mother, I suppose, and she was not ambitious in terms of a career. But she knew what she was good at — raising children and taking care of a home. And she did those things really well. Her home was always well cared for and she could control her children with a glance. I liked her.'

Rudolf was a seaport customs officer by profession, and was frequently transferred from one port to the next. Louise can no longer remember precisely when her aunt and uncle left Wismar for Cuxhaven, but she was aware that she had not seen, spoken to 'or even thought of the couple' for several years. She did not even know their address.

Still, they represented her only hope of not spending more hungry weeks wandering the countryside. She also wanted to avoid a possible further stint as a prisoner of the Allied forces, although, as she now jokingly admits, 'Locked up, at least you were fed every day. There were times when it didn't seem such a bad idea to be caught.'

For six days Louise walked along the dyke in the direction of Cuxhaven, part of a ragged diaspora of civilians and soldiers — some seeking a way back home, others searching for a safe place to make a new beginning.

On finally reaching the town, she was delighted to find it relatively unscathed — a startling sight given the vast stretches of destruction she had just travelled through.

'It looked like a normal city almost, there was very little damage. I'm not sure why it escaped the bombing; perhaps there were strategic reasons. I was so happy to see somewhere that was intact, where people seemed to have a chance to get on with their lives.

'Of course I had no idea where my relatives lived and I'd never been to Cuxhaven before in my life. Still, I had to start somewhere. I went to the town centre and just started asking people if they knew Rudolf and Elizabeth Fox. I stood there for several hours with no luck. Then I started asking people if there was any special housing for port customs employees. Luckily, there was, and I was given directions to it. Once I was at the right apartment block, it was fairly easy to track them down.'

Louise was knocking on her aunt and uncle's front door less than a day after arriving in Cuxhaven — no mean feat in an unfamiliar city of some 80,000 residents.

Despite having had limited contact with her relatives in recent years, Louise was confident they would offer to take her into their home.

'We were family, after all. Even though we hadn't spoken in some time, I wasn't worried about being turned away. I know I would have helped them if the situation had been reversed.'

She was right. Although being considerably taken aback by the unexpected sight of her by now rather travel-worn and weary niece standing on her doorstep, Lizbeth Fox welcomed her warmly and offered her shelter without hesitation.

Although her home and her city were intact, the war had delivered Lizbeth Fox a greater agony. Rudolf had been sent to fight on the eastern front and had not yet returned. All that his wife knew for certain was that he had been captured by the Russians and transported to a prisoner of war camp in Siberia some twelve months before.

Since then, she had heard nothing of his fate.

'My aunt was obviously concerned about her husband. So, in that regard, I think she was glad to have me around. I was company for her and I helped her look after her four children, who were all under school age. I would take them to the beach when the weather was warm — which wasn't often in Cuxhaven I am sorry to say; it is winter there about eleven months of the year, I think — and I helped her with the housework and shopping. Lizbeth would sometimes talk to me about her husband, about how upset and worried she was. She would cry often. She was very stressed, but still she kept the household running under very difficult circumstances.'

The Cuxhaven Foxes lived in a small three-bedroom apartment not far from the port itself. With the four children already assigned to two bedrooms, Louise and her aunt had little choice but to share a bedroom — an arrangement that at least kept them both a little warmer in a town renowned for its brutally cold climate and which, like the rest of the nation, was suffering from an acute shortage of coal.

Most of the country's significant coal resources had been gobbled up by the war effort or were unable to be processed because of the damage done to both infrastructure and manpower levels. The widespread destruction of railway lines and roads further exacerbated the crisis — even the coal that was available was often difficult to transport to areas in need. With cruel timing, the two winters following the German surrender in 1945 were amongst the coldest on record. The effects on an already battered population, weakened by hunger and the shock of defeat, were dire.

'People froze to death in their homes. In Cuxhaven I can remember hearing about the old people, especially — just found dead in their beds or even sitting in their chairs. Even two years after the war had ended, people were still victims of it. Life had become very brutal. The weakest did not survive and the stronger ones had to harden their hearts and get on with it. To stay warm, everything that could be burnt was burnt — people would go into the streets to scavenge for wood or even rags to burn. Of course, before long, there was nothing left.'

In 1946, in the middle of the first post-war winter, a certain Cardinal Frings, Archbishop of Cologne, declared in a sermon to the faithful that theft, in times of life-threatening emergency, was both understood and overlooked by God. Shortly thereafter, around 900 tons of coal per day began to mysteriously vanish from Cologne Railway Station. Train services were often interrupted as a result of fuel shortages, but it is assumed that at least some church-going Cologne residents kept themselves a little warmer at night. Stealing coal, wood and other fuel soon became known colloquially as a Fringsen in the cardinal's honour.[1]

The lack of coal caused the electricity supply to become haphazard and unreliable.

'In the first couple of years, we only had electricity some of the time. In the first few months after the war, there wasn't much power at all. It might only be on for an hour or two at a time, and there didn't seem to be any certainty about when it would turn on or when it would shut down. Later, they seemed to get a pattern going. It was usually on for a few hours in the morning and it would be off all night. We would get up and do all our cooking and preparations for the day in the morning while there was electricity. It became something that people adapted to.'

Much harder to accommodate however, were the ongoing and critical food shortages.

'We were all issued with ration cards of course, but there just wasn't much food available. Everything was in very short supply. Sometimes, word would get out that a certain shop was going to get a supply of meat or butter in the morning. Rumours would go around, everyone spent so much time thinking about and searching for enough food to eat for the day. When you heard a rumour like that, you would try to outsmart everyone else by turning up at the shop in the middle of the night, hoping to get near the front of the queue. Usually, when you got there, there would already be a long line of people standing quietly in the darkness, waiting for morning and the shop to open. Even in the snow, people would queue. Sometimes, the shop did have fresh meat or some other item that was scarce, but you usually had to be one of the first people in to get it. Other times, the rumours had been false and there was very little at all to buy.

'What I do remember was that what little meat we got during this time often looked strange. People said we were eating horse, sometimes even dog and cat. I'm convinced that was true. It certainly wasn't the normal meat that we were used to. But we didn't care. It was much better than starving. In parts of East Prussia we heard that people were so desperate for food that they had been forced to strip the bark off trees and eat it. Sometimes they ate grass. At least it hadn't come to that for us.

'And it wasn't only food that was scarce. For almost three years there was no clothing, or furniture, available; you could buy none of the items that people take for granted these days. If your skirt tore, you had to mend it. There was no shop to go and buy another one from.'

After taking a few months to recover from her trek, Louise realised the time had come to look for work. Cuxhaven was part of the British territorial zone — Britain, France and the US having carved Western Germany into three distinct regions, while Russia, of course, controlled much of the east — and the city's new administrators were keen to re-establish production and employment opportunities as quickly as possible.

'I wanted to help my aunt out by having some money to give her and of course I needed a job if I was to be able to afford an apartment of my own.'

With Cuxhaven filled with Allied troops and officials, Louise's ability to speak English should have put her in a good position to find work without much delay. The role she had played in the war, however, soon proved to be a distinct disadvantage.

At the conclusion of hostilities, Britain, France and the US had agreed that, within their zone of occupation, every German citizen would be made aware not only of the enormity of the crimes committed by Hitler, but also of the seriousness of their involvement in them.

The Allied De-Nazification Policy, as the programme became known, echoed the thoughts of US President Roosevelt, who had written as early as 1944 that the German people must 'have it driven into them' that they were involved — actively or by complicity — 'in a lawless conspiracy'.[2]

In Cuxhaven, as in all Allied controlled cities, no application for employment or social security benefits of any kind could be considered without the applicant first completing a 131-point questionnaire designed to gauge an individual's political affiliations and the amount of personal responsibility they bore for war crimes.

These forms were then examined and sorted into several categories. A citizen could either be exonerated — in which case they were free to work where they chose and to receive all entitlements available to them — or they could be classified according to a rather strange sliding scale devised by Allied bureaucrats. One could either be labelled a follower, a lesser offender, an offender or a major offender. Major offenders were put on trial and often jailed, while penalties varied for those who were deemed to fall into the other, less serious, categories.

Louise, who had applied for a secretarial job with the British army in their Shipbuilding Control Commission headquarters, made the mistake of filling out the forms truthfully.

'I tried to be accurate with the forms and of course, that was a bad idea. I don't know what I was classified as, but I was told I wasn't suitable to work for the British Army. And since the British and Americans were basically in charge of most jobs in Cuxhaven at that time, this was a serious problem for me.'

Wherever administrative red tape appears, sooner or later someone discovers a pair of scissors. In the case of the De-Nazification question-naire, those scissors took the form of an affidavit in which a third party could swear they were certain of the applicant's strong anti-Nazi sympathies. These affidavits, known as Persilschein (or laundry list —

the word Persil being derived from a popular brand of detergent) basically cleansed the applicant in the eyes of the overworked assessment officers. Priests were known to hand these sworn statements out, even to relative strangers, and there was also a thriving market in tailor-made affidavits written to specification.[3]

Louise recalls that these Persilschein however were generally favoured by high-ranking Nazi officials or former SS soldiers — those who faced potential arrest or, at the very least, an extended period of unemployment and exclusion should their former loyalties be revealed.

'I just waited six months or so and then reapplied. I filled in the same form — they obviously didn't keep the records for very long — and this time I lied. I don't remember now precisely what I wrote on the form, but I know I made no mention of having worked for Luftwaffe Supreme Command or for Goering. I didn't enjoy lying, but it was necessary.'

Louise's second application failed to arouse the suspicions of Allied pencil pushers and she was re-classified as a Nazi party follower rather than functionary. She was just one of countless Germans to slip through the gaping holes in the Allied De-Nazification net. Poorly organised and implemented, the program failed to flush out many Party officials or senior officers, most of whom had either the funds or the contacts to beat the system and avoid detection. Minor Nazi functionaries, foot soldiers and a few headstrong idealists formed the bulk of those prosecuted, and the entire program was deemed a comprehensive failure and scrapped by 1948.

After receiving her new classification, Louise promptly accepted a secretarial position at the Shipbuilding Control office, where the administration skills learnt serving the German air force were now put to use assisting the British army.

The irony of her new position did not escape her, but far from having any qualms about working for a former enemy, Louise was simply grateful to have paid employment once more. For most, the grinding hardship of life in post-war Germany had already elbowed aside all questions of loyalty or principle. Survival was everything.

'I can laugh about that job now; it seems funny, I know, that I went from working for one side to the other in a matter of months. But I didn't mind. The war was over and the British were mostly quite good people to work for. I needed the money and nobody was in a position to be too fussy.'

As the name suggests, the British Shipbuilding Control Commission had been hastily established to ensure that all German sea-going vessels were suitable only for non-military uses.

'The Allies were afraid that Germany would build up an army and a navy again, just as they had done after the First World War. The Commission's job was to check that any boat being built, or even a boat in need of repair, could not be used by Germany in a war. The building of naval ships was of course forbidden, but if you wanted to build a fishing boat or a tug boat for example, you had to have permission from the Commission. Every specification of that boat had to be approved — right down to the type of bolts used.

'The work was secretarial, typing, shorthand and so on. There wasn't much to do really. There were three girls working in the office and we had a lot of free time. It was quite boring actually, especially after all the long hours I had worked during the war. I didn't want to work that hard again of course, but I found it hard to go at such a slow pace. I think that the British were employing more people than they needed in some jobs — just to get people working again.

'My boss was Tommy O'Brien, an Irishman. He was quite pleasant, and would sometimes give us chocolate. The British soldiers usually had chocolate and cigarettes. For us, these things were rarer than gold. The Americans always had more than the British.

'One of the other benefits of the job was that we were given hot meals during the day. Food was still scarce, so having a meal provided was a real bonus. We were lucky really, compared to some.'

A full stomach however, soon proved to be just one of the advantages of working for the Shipbuilding Control Commission.

'One of the few German naval vessels that were permitted to continue operating — under Allied control, of course — were the minesweepers. They were necessary to remove all the mines floating off the German coast. A fleet of minesweepers was based at Cuxhaven; their job was to clear the North Sea. Now, these minesweepers had a supply of coal on board. Once I had been working at Shipbuilding Control for a few months, I realised that some of the staff there were doing black-market business with the sailors from the minesweepers. I soon joined in, as we were desperate for coal at home.

'I would collect chocolate, butter, cigarettes especially, whatever I could get my hands on. The British soldiers would give out cigarettes quite often — especially to girls who flirted with them — and I would keep mine for trading. Sometimes you would swap something on your ration card for another thing that was easier to trade with. At night, I would sneak down to the docks and swap these goods for coal with the sailors.

'I did this for several months — in fact there were quite a few people I worked with involved. It was going really well until, one day, the minesweepers couldn't operate because the sailors had sold all the coal on the black market. It meant a court martial for them and no more coal for us.'

By now, Louise had acquired a taste for black-market trading and, despite the episode with the luckless North Sea sailors and a likely gaol sentence if convicted, she entered the shadowy world of illegal trading with enthusiasm.

'They were desperate times and everyone did what they could to survive. A year or so after the war ended, a single cigarette was worth the equivalent of 10 British pounds in black-market currency; a pound of butter was worth 50 pounds. It was madness. Dances had started up again in Cuxhaven and I would go to them to have some fun but also in the hope of getting some cigarettes from the soldiers. The British were the nicest; we liked them the best. They were more modest than the Americans, who were often very arrogant and would show off. The British were usually gentlemen, too. But I would talk and dance with the soldiers and hope they would give me a cigarette. When they did, I hoarded them up.

'The black market in Cuxhaven was based in the waiting room of the railway station. The trains weren't running then, and there was never any electricity on at night. It was the perfect place, deserted and dark. People would quietly sneak in and then walk around with candles, seeing what everyone had to offer and trying to bargain with them. Sometimes, there'd be soldiers there; they would use their ration of cigarettes or chocolate and swap it for money or for some particular item they couldn't get from the military. The people in that waiting room came from all levels of society — rich, poor, whatever.

'One night, I had come to sell some cigarettes for bread. With four children at home, Lizbeth and I were always in need of food. Suddenly, a spotlight was turned on and we could hear voices yelling at everyone to stay where they were. Of course, everyone did just the opposite. People climbed out of windows, tried to crawl out through the rear door on their hands and knees — everyone was desperate to get out of there. I didn't make it, and was arrested. I spent a few days in prison waiting for my trial. I loved it there, it was warm and they gave you three meals a day. I hadn't had three regular meals a day for a couple of years. When I had to go before the judge at my trial, I was in for a shock. As soon as I saw him, I realised he looked familiar. I had seen him before — in the disused railway station. I'd sold him cigarettes. I glared at him while he read out my sentence — I could tell he remembered me too. He sentenced me to three weeks, but in truth, I didn't mind at all. Oh, the food — I never wanted to leave. I was very disappointed when they released me.'

The early post-war years were also a time when family connections severed by the vagaries of conflict were finally resolved — sometimes happily, often not. For many families — including the Foxes — even survival against the odds sometimes proved to be a mixed blessing.

Several months after she selflessly agreed to take in her niece, Lizbeth Fox received the message she had been praying for. Her husband had not only survived internment in Siberia, but had been released by the Russians and was now being kept at a recovery camp near Hamburg.

'Lizbeth was told she had to catch a train to Hamburg and collect Rudolf. I stayed at home and looked after the children. She was very excited, but also nervous I think. When she returned a few days later I was shocked to see my uncle. He was so weak and thin, he couldn't walk. Lisbeth had to virtually carry him off the train; he could hardly stand by himself. He was only in his thirties but he looked much older.'

Both women were initially hopeful that Rudolf would eventually recover from his trauma, but the few details he revealed to Louise about his experience at the hands of the Russians and of the brutal Siberian climate soon made it clear that the extent of his suffering had been formidable.

'He never talked about what happened to him very much. And, of course, I didn't want to press the issue, we didn't want to upset him. Perhaps he told his wife more, I don't know. I do recall him telling us how the prisoners were so hungry that they would scavenge through the rubbish bins, looking for scraps. How they had eaten virtually anything they could get their hands on, no matter how disgusting. Once they found some old fish heads and tails in the bin. They ate them raw. Of course, we were hungry too, we often had nothing more to eat than some deep fried potato peels. But what he had suffered — we couldn't even imagine it.'

Lizbeth's relief at her husband's homecoming proved to be fleeting. Two months after he returned from Siberia, Rudolf Fox died of stomach cancer. Louise has no doubt that the internment was the primary cause of his early death.

'Being starved, being cold, being beaten all the time — I think that was what triggered his illness. He was a casualty of war too — even though he didn't die on a battlefield.'

Soon after she arrived in Cuxhaven, Louise had also initiated a search for her missing parents and sister through the Red Cross. Six months later she received the reply she had hardly dared to dream of — Fritz, Lucy and Gerda Fox had all survived the war and were back living in Wismar.

'I was very happy to know they were all okay, although they had been through a great deal like all of us. And, of course, Wismar was now controlled by the Russians so that was another problem.'

Aerial bombing and the enthusiastic vandalism of the often ill-disciplined Russian soldiers had devastated Wismar. Like large areas of the town, the Foxes' old apartment block had been reduced to rubble and they were briefly homeless before being taken in by Louise and Gerda's former piano teacher.

'They had absolutely nothing apart from the few possessions they had managed to bring with them from Gdansk. Not a single stick of furniture survived from our old apartment. It took them a long time before they were even able to move out of my piano teacher's home. Eventually they found another flat which they shared with some other people — very crowded, very basic. But they survived, and within a couple of years, my father had rejoined the orchestra and was working again. My mother got a job eventually as well.

'Life under the Russians was hard though. One night my father was walking home from a concert. He carried a violin and a saxophone that he had played during the performance. Some Russians soldiers found him — they were drunk as usual — and attacked him. When he finally made it home he was wearing nothing but his underpants and his instruments had been stolen. Those Russians had taken his clothes for themselves and I suppose took his instruments to sell or just to destroy for fun. They were very violent and brutal, the Russians; they were a completely different culture from us Germans or even from the English. They were feared.

'Of course, for my father, those instruments were his livelihood. I remember sending money so he could buy new instruments. It was a terrible thing to do, especially to such a harmless man minding his own business.'

Despite the additional difficulties imposed by the Russian regime, Louise's parents had little interest in leaving Wismar to try their luck elsewhere, even though leaving what would soon become known as East Germany was still possible, at least in the Baltic region.

'No, they didn't want to leave, even though life was hard. They were getting older and Wismar was their home after all. Despite everything, it was where they felt most comfortable. My sister did leave though — she ended up getting out of Wismar while you still could. Later she met an American soldier, married him and went to live in America.'

Fritz and Lucy would finally bow to the inevitable and divorce that same year. They would both remain in Wismar for the rest of their lives, their separation offering them both a degree of happiness unattainable during their marriage. Fritz would find new love and Lucy achieved some of that independence and career success she had always yearned for. Whilst she remained in contact with both until their deaths, Louise never saw either of her parents again.

By 1947, Louise had moved out of Lisbeth Fox's apartment in response to Rudolf's return and found a place of her own. For the reasonable sum of 20 marks a week she secured her own furnished room complete with shared kitchen and bathroom.

With her own flat and an independent income, Louise felt able to resume some semblance of normal living, despite the continued food and clothing and power shortages.

'I had a few boyfriends, but they didn't stay long. Some left because of the weather in Cuxhaven; they couldn't stand the rough climate. Also, many people were still moving around at this time, they were taking temporary jobs or maybe moving from place to place because they had lost everything in the war and wanted to start again.

'I went out with a few British soldiers — I spoke enough English to have a conversation with them and, of course, talking with them improved my English even further. I went to dances, occasionally drank some rum if I could find any. I tried to enjoy myself as much as I could but it was difficult. I also found it hard to really trust anyone any more. I was always suspicious of people's motives. I hadn't been like that before.'

However, she did develop enough trust in others to finally throw away the cyanide pill given to her at Berchtesgaden almost three years earlier — and seemed somewhat surprised when I asked why she had held on to such a grim memento for so long.

'Well, I had to be sure I wouldn't need it. There was a part of me that still worried about what would happen. I needed the pill just in case.'

It was in that same year that Louise claims she first became fully aware of the existence of concentration camps and the mass extermination of Jews and others deemed racially inferior by the Nazis.

'The Allies distributed our ration cards. One day we were told we would not receive our cards until we had gone to see a particular film. So, of course, we went — nobody wanted to starve — and I can remember sitting in the cinema at Cuxhaven waiting in the dark for the film to begin and thinking how I was wasting my time watching some stupid propaganda.'

But when she saw the black and white images of emaciated concentration camp survivors, of military trucks with stiffened corpses stacked in the back like firewood, of crematoriums where human bones jutted from beneath piles of ash, Louise's annoyance turned to shock.

'What we were seeing was horrible. Nobody could believe it. The film said that all of this had been done by the Nazis and that we should be ashamed of it. That the Russians had found some people in the camps so starved and ill that they had shot them and put them out of their misery, like animals.'

The film quickly became a central talking point and generated a wide range of opinions and reactions amongst Louise's acquaintances.

'At first, most people said they didn't believe any of it. The view was that it was just propaganda invented by the Allies as an excuse to make us feel bad and to give them a legitimate reason for coming into the war and causing so much destruction in Germany. Every person I spoke to about it said the same thing — how can these things have happened when we knew nothing about it?

'But gradually, as time went on and we received more information about what had happened, people began to realise it was the truth. And it was a terrible thing to know — that something like this had been done in Germany's name. Of all the lies that Hitler told us, this one was the biggest and the worst.'

The relative guilt of the German population in regard to the concentration camps has long been a contentious and emotionally loaded issue.

In his bestselling book, *Hitler's Willing Executioners: Ordinary Germans and the Holocaust*, academic Daniel J Goldhagen argues strongly in support of his theory that the mass murder of Jews was largely the result of the intense anti-Semitism of the German population. Hitler, Goldhagen claims, was merely carrying out the popular wish of his people. This widespread hatred of the Jews also allowed men without any combat or even prior military experience to carry out grisly executions day after day, without any apparent moral conflict.

A demonological anti-Semitism, of the virulent racial variety, was the common structure of the perpetrator's cognition and of German society in general. The German perpetrators ... were assenting mass executioners, men and women who, true to their own eliminationist anti-Semitic beliefs, faithful to their cultural anti-Semitic credo, considered the slaughter to be just.[4]

Hans Fritzche, head of the news section of Goebbels' Press Division, argued at Nuremberg in defence of his fellow citizens and their knowledge of the concentration camps.

I am firmly convinced that the German people were unaware of the mass murders of the Jews and the assertions to that effect were considered rumours, and reports which reached the German people from outside were officially denied again and again.

If the German people had learned of these mass murders, they would certainly no longer have supported Hitler. They would probably have sacrificed five million for a victory, but never would the German people have wished to bring about victory by the murder of five million people.[5]

Fritzche, one of the few high-ranking Nazis found not guilty at Nuremberg, had every reason to be both self-serving and highly selective in his trial testimony. However, his belief in a populace largely ignorant of the existence of Hitler's Final Solution receives more credible support from a document issued from the Führer's headquarters on 11 July 1943 and headed *Re: Treatment of the Jewish Question.*

On instructions from the Führer I make known the following: where the Jewish question is brought up in public, there may be no discussion of a future overall solution (Gesamtlösung). It may, however, be mentioned that the Jews are taken in groups for appropriate labour purposes.[6]

In April 1945, the esteemed *Life* magazine photographer Margaret Bourke-White was on hand when US Forces liberated the Buchenwald concentration camp, where it is estimated at least 50,000 people died. Her chilling account of what took place when Americans forced residents of the nearby city of Weimar to walk through the camps to witness for themselves the atrocities that had been committed, in many ways encapsulates both sides of the argument.

> Women fainted. Men covered their faces and turned their heads away. When the civilians cried out again and again, 'We didn't know. We didn't know,' the liberated prisoners were besides themselves with fury. 'You knew,' they screamed.[7]

Even sixty years on, the debate continues.

After almost a decade of economic winter, 1948 offered a dazzling taste of spring.

The Marshall Plan, named after the US Secretary of State George C. Marshall and introduced by the Allies in an attempt to regenerate the wounded economies of Europe, injected some US$13 billion (around US$65 billion today) into several countries, including Germany. The aim was to promote the European production and manufacturing sector, bolster devastated currencies, facilitate international trade and create new markets for US goods. The Americans had learned the lessons of Weimar well.

Abandoning Germany would merely encourage anti-western sentiment to fester and spread and present the Soviets with a prime opportunity to extend their influence. A prosperous and economically powerful Germany, on the other hand, would be nullified as a future enemy and, with its well-educated and diligent workforce, offered tremendous prospects for future development.

Between 1948 and 1952, the Marshall Plan changed the face of Germany forever.

'One day, they simply took all our old money and handed us back new money. We all got the same amount per person. Instantly, the shops that had been empty for years were suddenly full of things to buy. I don't know how they managed to get things in stock so quickly. It was like a dream. Everyone was so happy, so thrilled to have something to spend money on. There were clothes and furniture — even chocolate. I never ate so much chocolate in my life! It had been this rare thing, this great luxury for so long and now it was in all the shops and I had money to just go in and buy as much as I wanted!

'Of course, the Americans had to spoil things a little by introducing us to the hire purchase scheme. Germans had never had such a thing before. For the first time, you could buy now and pay later. Imagine, people who had nothing but a wobbly chair for years now had the chance to buy lots of furniture and not even pay for it all at once. A lot of people went a bit crazy and got into real financial trouble.

'But for me, I only went crazy for chocolate, and probably a bit for clothes, too. But I didn't go too far. My life started to feel almost normal again. I was working, I had a place to live, and there was money and things to spend it on. It was a nice feeling after so much sadness and suffering.'

For the next seven years Louise remained in Cuxhaven, content if uninspired by her job and her lifestyle. While not exactly happy, she was at least safe, fed and relatively stress-free.

'There is not much I can say about this period of my life. It was a rather dull time for me. I worked in the same job, with the same people. I had my little apartment and a small circle of friends. I went out when I could and enjoyed myself wherever possible.

'For Germany though, it was a very exciting time. In areas where the aerial bombing campaign had been severe, millions of dollars and thousands of man hours were being poured in to rebuilding and repairing infrastructure. Whole cities were being virtually rebuilt from the ground up. We had to start almost from scratch — we needed new railways, new roads, new office buildings, new homes. Water, sewerage, gas and electricity — even these basic services had to be restored to huge areas of the country. The newspapers were filled with reports of new building work, of the speed at which Germany was repairing itself. In fact, ten years after the war ended, there were very few places left in Germany where you could still see major damage from the fighting. That's how quickly Germans got on with the task, how hard everyone worked. It was a remarkable achievement really, particularly for a nation that had been so badly defeated and demoralised.

'In Cuxhaven, the pace was a little slower. The town had hardly been damaged at all by the war, so not much rebuilding needed to be done. But new shops and services started opening fairly quickly after 1948 — as people realised that they didn't need to leave the country, that there was a future for everyone in Germany. So even Cuxhaven became bigger, more lively. After a while the bars and restaurants started up and people began to have fun again. Life still wasn't exactly the same as it had been before the war of course, but it was getting back to normal faster than I think anyone could have imagined under the circumstances.

'In some ways, it was probably necessary to have this stability after all the dramas of the previous years. I know at first it was wonderful to just have a normal routine and to not live in fear of being bombed or captured or shot at. I'm sure most Germans felt the same way. Boring was good, for a while. But as the years passed, I began to feel restless again. The stability of my life had now become dull. I wasn't desperate for a man, but it would have been nice, I suppose. I wasn't getting any younger — already I was past what would have been considered a marriageable age in those days. Of course, I was not alone in this. Men were very hard to find. After a while, I started to wonder if this was how I was going to live out the rest of my life. And I knew I wanted something more. I had only come to Cuxhaven by chance, in a moment of desperation, and now years later, I was still there. I wanted something to happen. I wanted a change. But I didn't know how to make that happen.'

Then along came a letter from Else Klinkov, a friend from her air force days. Else and Louise had been in regular contact since the end of the war. It was the offer of a job working with Else in Frankfurt that jolted Louise into action and offered the opportunity for her to embark on yet another of what she calls her 'little adventures'.

'Else said she could get me a job working with her in an office. It was a grain import company, not exciting it's true, but what I was doing in Cuxhaven wasn't very interesting either. In Frankfurt, I believed I had more opportunities; it was much larger, the climate was better, and all the money that had been flowing into Germany from the Marshall Plan was even more evident in the larger cities. I decided Frankfurt was just the change I needed.'

In typical fashion Louise left Cuxhaven — her haven and home for a decade — with few regrets, a minimum of fuss and with her thoughts already focused on the future.

7 NEW BEGINNINGS

To dare is to lose one's footing momentarily.
To not dare is to lose oneself.
Søren Kierkegaard

FRANKFURT SOON PROVED to be a mistake.

It was not that the city failed to offer the change of pace that Louise yearned for — despite extensive bombing Frankfurt had demonstrated a remarkable capacity for regeneration and by Louise's arrival an extensive rebuilding program was already under way and the city's cinemas, theatres and opera houses were bustling with patrons once again.

Both her accommodation — a furnished room in the middle-class suburb of Bornheim — and her social life — largely thanks to Else — were perfectly adequate. What really troubled Louise were the excessive demands of her new job and the fact that despite her now being in her mid thirties, there was still no committed male companion in her life.

The Marshall Plan had kick-started the German economy to a degree that perhaps not even its designers had anticipated. The German people had both money and opportunity and a rapidly growing optimism that, this time, there would be a lasting peace in which to savour both. While Louise was far from immune from the enthusiasm that was surging through all levels of German society, the boom also meant a workload which began to rival those mad Luftwaffe days.

'After a year or so in Frankfurt, I found that I was always tired. My life involved too much work and not enough sleep. I worked six days a week in the grain import office, doing administrative tasks. It was dull and the hours were very long. It got to the stage where I just spent my weekends in bed, too tired to get out. Sometimes I would go into the office on Sunday afternoon — my one day off — just to prepare some paperwork that had to be done on Monday morning. The job took over my life. I'd already experienced that in the Luftwaffe and I knew the damage working those sorts of hours can do. But at least then it was an extraordinary time, a special set of circumstances. This wasn't wartime, it was just a job.

'I suppose I was lonely, too, although I think I would have coped better with everything else if I hadn't been so worn down from work. You must remember Germany had lost millions of men to the war. Finding someone who was the right age or who wasn't crippled or in some way damaged by the war was very difficult. A lot of men, especially those who had made money, started to have girlfriends as well as a wife. It became quite common. These wealthy men realised they were in a very privileged situation and they took full advantage of it. The poor women had very little choice but to put up with it. The wives were terrified of being abandoned with no money, while the girlfriends were just happy to be spoilt. Very often the girlfriends were treated better than the wife, who usually had to look after the children and do housework while the mistress was put in a nice apartment somewhere and showered with gifts.'

Such was the extent of the gender imbalance that German legislators at one point gave serious consideration to changing the law to allow a man to be legally married to more than one woman at a time.

By 1958, constant physical exhaustion and mental torment had reduced Louise to a black state of mind she recalls as being 'almost suicidal'.

So demanding had her schedule become that Louise — always an avid reader — now found that her regular late Saturday afternoon session at the hairdressers provided one of her few opportunities to sit and relax with a good book. On one particular Saturday it was not some worthy tome but an English-language magazine — bought with the aim of improving her written language skills — that held her attention underneath the hair dryer.

'There was an advertisement encouraging people to write to penfriends around the world. You had to write some details about yourself, plus send ten Australian pounds to an address in Sydney. The mention of Australia really got my interest. To me, it was another planet. I couldn't think of anywhere less familiar and more remote. The advertisement said that in return for the money, you would be sent the addresses of some people they thought matched you in some way, and you could start to write to them.

'In an instant, this crazy idea popped into my head. I would take up this offer and find some penpals.

'I sat there and thought, why not? What have I got to lose? I was depressed, I was tired. My life didn't seem to have any purpose. Writing a letter was such a small thing; I didn't really think anything would come of it.'

Before long, Louise was in regular correspondence with three men from very different parts of the globe — one from Wales, another from Japan, a third from Argentina.

While she enjoyed the letters and learning about life in far-flung places, she thought of her penpals as nothing more than a hobby, a mild distraction from the monotony of the everyday. Until she received a letter from John Barnes.

'One afternoon this letter arrived out of the blue. It was from a man named John who had been given my details from the penpal agency in Australia. His letter was light-hearted and quite funny. He struck me immediately as an interesting, friendly sort of person. He told me he came from Tasmania — Launceston to be precise. I didn't even know where it was. I got out the atlas after his first letter arrived and searched for it. When I saw this little tiny place on the map I just laughed. Oh my God, I thought, it's so small, why do they even bother?'

Still, there was something intriguing about this jovial sounding man who came from a part of the world that was utterly unfamiliar. Louise decided to write back, and before long a regular correspondence had developed between the two.

'I liked his letters, the way he wrote, the things he said. He was funny and very easy-going. He didn't try hard to impress me, he wasn't a braggart. I liked that. He seemed very natural, a man you could talk to very easily. Of course, there were still so many differences between us. There were problems with both language and, of course, culture. For instance, when I asked him what he did for a living he told me he was a bookmaker. I assumed that was someone who made books. I didn't know any better. When I asked him did he make the books by hand, he thought that was very funny.'

The couple exchanged pictures and before too long, John became Louise's sole penpal. Despite their easy rapport, Louise was still completely taken aback when, some six months after they first started writing to one another, John wrote and suggested that Louise come and see Tasmania for herself.

'He said, would you consider coming here and seeing if you like it? He would pay my fare — first class — as well as all my other travelling expenses. He would organise the paperwork to allow me to come to Australia. If I didn't like it, he would send me home any time I wanted. I must have read that letter a thousand times. It was an enormous surprise to me. But, do you know, even though it took me some time to make up my mind definitely, I considered moving to Australia as a definite possibility from the moment I first opened that letter. I can see in hindsight that I was in desperate need of a major change in my life.

'People always say to me now, what a hard decision that must have been for you. And it was in many ways. I was taking a big risk — the biggest one of my life. My friends thought I was mad. They told me that it was just a trick and that in Australia they would sell me to the white slave trade. They really thought that was true. But all these people telling me not to go only made me more pigheaded. I thought — why not go and see what happens? I was very unhappy in Frankfurt and there didn't seem to be much hope that things would change soon. This was a chance for me to see the world and have an adventure, if nothing else. Life was for living, and I wanted to start living it again. So I took a deep breath and crossed my fingers; I wrote to John and told him yes.'

Six months later, Louise was aboard the aptly named SS *Australia*, travelling in style and completely exhilarated at her first foray into the world outside Germany.

'I spent four weeks on board that ship. It was very crowded, but John has given me a first-class ticket, so it was fine. The ship stopped at so many places; oh God, they were all fascinating. We caught the ship in Genoa and picked up passengers along the Italian coast, then we went to Colombo in Sri Lanka, Jakarta in Indonesia ... these were different worlds for me and I was fascinated. We didn't have the opportunity to stop very long in any one place, but I took every chance I could get to explore. I tried to take in as much as I could — the sights, the smells, the sounds, the colours of a new country. I had lived a very sheltered existence in some ways. Yes, I'd had adventures and been through a lot of suffering, but I had never seen the world outside my own country. Even before I arrived in Australia, I felt that perhaps — finally — I was starting to live my life on my own terms and in my own style.'

Louise Fox took her first step on Australian soil at midnight on a chilly Melbourne evening.

'There wasn't much to see at that stage. It was dark and cold, raining in fact. Walking down that crowded gangplank I was nervous of course, but also exhilarated. A million thoughts were going through my head that night; some good, some bad. But at least I felt alive.'

Waiting for her on the dock was a man she had never met but already counted as a friend. John Barnes was a divorced 52-year-old bookmaker from Launceston, Tasmania. Attractive in a rough-hewn, knockabout sort of way — wavy blond hair touched with grey and a face well suited to smiling — Barnes was a well-known figure in the small community of Launceston. He was fond of a drink, a joke and the company of others.

Louise was somewhat overwhelmed by the journey and the barrage of unfamiliar sights and sounds that greeted her as she disembarked, and the sight of John's familiar face in the crowd offered no small comfort.

'Of course, I was still wondering if I had done the right thing. Although I liked John, we didn't really know each other. Letters are not the same as seeing someone face-to-face. But I was also excited. Here I was in Australia — who would have believed it?'

For Louise, Launceston initially proved to be no less exotic and surreal than the steaming coastal jungles of Sri Lanka.

'I found it all very different. Language and customs — these differences I'd expected, and although they caused problems, they didn't surprise me. It was the little things that I found strangest at first. Driving on the left-hand side of the road — that took me a long time to get used to. And Launceston was so hilly. Wismar and Cuxhaven are both very flat; the last time I had seen mountains was in Berchtesgaden. I've never felt like I belong in a hilly place, for some reason.

'The houses looked very different too — a different design, and the windows seemed so big. In Germany the windows are smaller because of the cold and snow. Here, the windows looked huge to me.

'Another thing was that there was no coffee in Launceston. I searched everywhere, but could only find tea. I had thought only the

English liked tea so much; I didn't realise that Australians were the same ... It took me months to finally find a shop that sold coffee beans. But by then I had got used to tea anyway.'

Thankfully for Louise, her relationship with John proved less troublesome.

'We got along very well, right from the beginning. In person, he was very much the way he came across in his letters. He was a kind, gentle sort of man. Intelligent and quick-witted, but he was always modest about it. I liked him very much. We were well suited, I think. We both wanted companionship, we were both lonely in our way. The arrangement worked out very well indeed.'

John Barnes lived on a large block of land on the outskirts of Launceston. He was an animal lover, and the property had a large aviary out the back, which quickly became one of Louise's responsibilities. He also introduced Louise to some of Tasmania's more elusive habitats, taking her on bush walks to find kangaroos, koalas and reptiles.

A gregarious man by nature and necessity (popularity being one of the best ways for small town bookmakers to distinguish themselves from their competitors at the track), Barnes was a man with many friends and even more acquaintances. Visitors came frequently, and when word spread that not only had a woman taken up residence, but one who was a foreigner, a *German* to boot, there were even more of them.

Louise quickly found herself the subject of much local curiosity and a great deal of not-so-subtle scrutiny.

'Everyone was very keen to meet me. Launceston was a small place, not much happened there, I suppose. So I was a novelty. People would come and ask me questions. But my English was not so good then. And people would talk so fast, I couldn't keep up. I would only be able to understand every second or third word they said. By the time I'd made sense of the question, they'd already have started talking about something else.

'The language problems made me shy. Also, I still felt very self-conscious. I was an outsider and that made me nervous. To be honest, I had always had a lack of self-confidence. I blame my mother for that. But at least in Germany I didn't have language problems and I knew what to do. Here, everything was so different. I didn't enjoy having to meet all these people. I would have preferred to hide in the kitchen or something, but that was usually impossible. It wasn't that I was unfriendly, but trying to hold a conversation in a language you are only just beginning to master is exhausting.'

Given that the war was still painfully fresh in the minds of most, Louise had anticipated some negative response to her nationality. But none was forthcoming, at least not to her knowledge.

'No, nobody in Launceston ever said anything about the Nazis to me. Maybe behind my back ... but I was never made to feel bad about it. In fact, most were curious and would ask me all sorts of questions. When I told them about my walk to Cuxhaven, and having met Goering and Hitler, they were amazed. I think they respected me actually. It was not a topic that I would raise myself, but if people asked me questions about my past, I would tell them the truth. I did not feel I had anything to be ashamed of. I never have.'

After years spent enduring one crisis after another, Louise relished the unhurried, gentle rhythm of her new life and worked hard to overcome the differences that set her apart from John's friends and neighbours.

'It wasn't a case of trying to escape my old life. I just wanted to embrace my new one. I knew that the better my English was and the more I understood about the Australian way of life, the quicker I could settle down in Launceston.'

It was a quiet existence by any standards — apart from the companionship she offered John Barnes, her other duties were fairly routine — housework, tending the aviary, grocery shopping. Despite being completely reliant financially — and to a large extent emotionally — on John, after four years Louise found herself gradually feeling at home in Tasmania and certain that she would not return to Germany.

'I got settled in Launceston after a while; I liked it. Before I'd arrived, I'd told myself I could always return to Germany if things didn't work out. But once I got used to Australia I knew that I didn't have any desire to go back to Germany. There was nothing for me there any more and there were too many bad memories left behind. Australia was my new home.'

Louise's loyalty to her adopted country suffered its first real test when John Barnes died unexpectedly of a heart attack.

'I was very shocked. It all happened so suddenly. He was never even ill, really. There was no warning. One day John was there and the next he was gone. I had been out shopping. I came home and found him lying on the living room floor. It was clear to me that he was already dead. I ran to the neighbours for help. They came rushing, and took over really. I felt very helpless. They rang the ambulance for me, even though it was obvious there was no point. They took him away and that was the last time I ever saw him.

'John's death was a terrible thing. And of course, it left me all alone. I had nothing. John and I were not married; it was not something he wanted to do and it didn't worry me either way. I felt like he was my husband, but I had never needed a formal arrangement for that. I was grateful for all he had given me. We had just been happy together and that had been more than enough. But back then, of course, not being his legal wife meant that I had no entitlement to any of his assets. He left nothing for me in his will. He had a grown-up daughter, and she got everything. I didn't know what to do. I had to move out of the house. I had no money of my own. John had given me money to buy food and so on and occasionally he would give me a little extra if he'd had a good day at the track. So basically I had to start out all over again.'

The dogged resilience that had been such a feature of Louise's character in the past was reawakened by this new crisis.

'I was terrified at first. My home was gone, I hardly had any money. I had only been in Australia for four years and was just beginning to feel like I belonged here. But after John's death, Australia started to feel like a foreign country all over again. Without John to help me, I felt very alone and vulnerable.

'I thought long and hard about returning to Germany at that point. It seemed the most logical thing to do. The problem was I didn't have enough money to get there. If I had had the fare back, I think I would be living in Germany now. But I was broke, and I really had no one to borrow the money from. Going back would also mean all my old friends could say "I told you so". And I didn't want that to happen. I was too pigheaded to allow them to be right. I also knew that all the aspects of German life that I had grown tired of were still there. In fact, those things had probably become even worse in my absence. The climate, the overcrowding of European cities, the more rushed pace of life. In Australia I had found a place that had very few of those problems — at least not then. I was reluctant to sacrifice what I loved about my new country just to return to my old one.

'It didn't take too long before I realised I had to do something to help myself. It wasn't as if I had never experienced grief or fear before. I had endured terrible hardships, and this wasn't the worst of them. It was difficult for me, but I gathered all my strength together and decided to get on with things.'

She quickly found herself a flat and a job selling Volkswagen cars at a Launceston dealership, a position she came to enjoy.

'I got to be quite good at it. It was fun really. I think perhaps my German accent got me the job in the first place — they probably thought I gave the dealership a more authentic touch since they were selling German cars. It was unusual for a woman to sell cars in those days too, so perhaps I was a novelty.

'The job really helped me improve my English — I was forced to speak to people and had to be able to reply quickly. It was good for me. I got to meet many of the locals too. And, most important, it helped me to gain more self-confidence. I was a strong-minded and strong-willed person, but not necessarily one that liked herself very much. Having to fend for myself, having to work and pay rent and sell cars — all those things enabled me to become more contented with who I was. I began to feel pride in myself and in the things I had achieved. And the things I had survived and overcome back in Germany. It was a nice feeling, after so many years.'

For a time it seemed she had emerged relatively unscathed from yet another personal upheaval. In reality though, the death of John Barnes would mark the beginning of one of the bleakest periods of Louise's life.

'I worked for the car firm for several years. The only problem with it was that the pay wasn't very good. But my choices were so limited in Launceston. I had to take what I could get. At least I was able to earn a living. I had friends of my own, a place to live and I was happy enough. I also had friends from Wismar who — believe it or not — lived in Wollongong. One day they went for a holiday to Sydney and I met up with them there. I'd never been to Sydney before, and I just fell in love with it. Oh, the ocean and the beaches and the climate — it was magical to me. I went back to Launceston at the end of the holiday and resigned immediately. I have never been one to hesitate when I am certain of something. I had learned how short and uncertain life can be, so I disliked lost opportunities. I made up my mind instantly — I was going to move to Sydney.'

Enamoured of the harbour city's beauty and confident that Sydney offered better employment prospects, Louise rented a small apartment near Bondi Beach and found work in the administrative office at a car repair firm. A few months later she slipped down a flight of stairs in her apartment block, breaking her ankle. The break was a serious one, requiring a long convalescence. Louise's new employers were less than understanding. She was fired and, less than 12 months after she left Tasmania, Louise returned to Launceston, dispirited and on crutches.

For a year Louise remained incapacitated and was forced to exist on sickness and unemployment benefits. When the ankle finally healed, her former employers at the Launceston car dealership agreed to reemploy her and she gratefully resumed her old job. If her life's journey seemed to have returned to an all too familiar holding pattern, at least it was a comfortable and quietly reassuring one.

Then, one day, while walking in a local park during her lunch break, Louise realised there was something wrong with her eyes.

'I was looking at some flowers, admiring them. Suddenly, everything went blurry. I rubbed my eyes, and my vision went back to normal. But it started happening again later on. My eyesight would be fine and then, without warning, everything would go fuzzy. I'd never had any eye problems before, but I assumed I just needed glasses. I went to the eye clinic and had tests. They told me there was nothing wrong with my eyes.

'So, I continued to put up with vision problems. After a few months, I started getting headaches — bad ones. I became really moody and depressed. I was having trouble controlling my emotions. I was aware that something was wrong, but I didn't seem able to think clearly. I was confused all the time. I couldn't think straight.'

Louise's behaviour became increasingly erratic. She began to experience aggressive mood swings and became verbally abusive to friends and work colleagues.

'I would start arguments over stupid little things. If the boss told me to do something that I didn't feel like, I would tell him off. I started using foul language, something I normally never did. At first, I was aware that I had done something wrong — I would yell at someone and then, later on, wonder why I had done so. But, as the weeks went by, I stopped even noticing my behaviour. I couldn't comprehend that

I was doing something wrong. To me, everyone deserved what they got. I felt filled with rage and confusion at everyone and everything around me. I can't recall if anyone there ever asked me what was wrong. They probably did. But I didn't think I was doing anything wrong. That was the problem.'

Unable to accommodate her bizarre behaviour, the Launceston car yard fired her.

'I think they tolerated me as long as they possibly could. I had worked there for a long time, and they liked me. But in the end, they just couldn't take it any more. How could I sell cars and deal with customers in my state? When they fired me, I didn't even care. It just made me angrier. I'm sure I probably abused them and stormed out. I was beginning to lose my common sense, my basic ability to reason, by that time.'

Louise applied for unemployment benefits, but soon became too disorganised in her thinking to even remember to pick up the cheques.

'Whole periods of time started to become blanks to me. It was as if I was sleepwalking even though I was awake. I stopped opening my mail, or I would open it and read it and then forget what it said. I didn't prepare proper meals any more — just ate out of cans or grabbed whatever was handy. I obviously started receiving letters about the rent not being paid, but I have no recollection of them. Finally, one day, they came and threw me out of the flat.'

Evicted from her apartment for non-payment of rent, Louise found herself reduced to vagrancy, living in local parks and sleeping outdoors even in the middle of Launceston's icy winters.

'The park seemed like the only option for me. It never occurred to me that I should seek help, or that it wasn't right for me to be living like this. I was no longer capable of that kind of reasoning.'

She had, by her own admission, become something of a madwoman.

'I had become so aggressive that I had taken to attacking strangers. I would yell at people walking past me — terrible things I would shout, swearwords and such. I actually hit and kicked some people. I stole too — did strange things on impulse. I remember going into a shop and stealing some lollies from the counter. I ran outside with the lollies and the owner caught me. I wasn't even ashamed or sorry — I just abused him.'

Having lived and worked in Launceston for so many years, Louise had a large circle of friends and acquaintances, some dating back to her days with John Barnes. Despite her obvious distress and the inexplicable change in her personality, not a single one offered her any help.

'In fact, they would cross to the other side of the street if they saw me coming. Of course, I had said terrible things to most of them, too, but it has always surprised and disappointed me that nobody tried to help. Nobody tried to find out what was wrong with me. They all just deserted me.'

Her decline reached its nadir when she was picked up by the police and arrested for vagrancy.

'I had caused too many problems, you see — always shouting and swearing at people. They just thought I was this crazy woman. I went before the judge and he was lecturing me. While he was talking, I fainted. I'd started to faint quite a bit. But by then I was in no condition to care about things like that. I wasn't able to think logically at all. The judge said he would send me to prison if I got caught sleeping in the park again. I just screamed at him too.

'And, of course, I got arrested again for vagrancy soon after. I didn't have anywhere else to go. What choice did I have? Anyway, they didn't send me to gaol and I probably wouldn't have cared even if they had.'

One day a nursing sister arrived in the park where Louise was living and insisted she accompany her to Launceston Hospital.

'I had hurt myself somehow earlier on — I can't even remember the details now — and I had been seen by a doctor. This doctor had been

curious about my behaviour and he suspected there was something physically wrong with me, that I wasn't just an eccentric. When he realised I
was living in the park, he had sent the nurse over to find me. Of course,
I had no intention of going anywhere. I screamed at the nurse, told her to
get away from me. She left and returned with the police. They had to
handcuff me and take me to the hospital by force. I kicked and spat at
them the whole time. I was like a lunatic.'

Brain scans soon revealed a two-year-old tumour.

'They never told me what size it was, and I probably didn't even
care enough to ask at that stage. I had very little sense of reality left.
They told me I would have to have an operation. They were going to
fly me to Melbourne. If the tumour was cancerous, I was obviously
going to die. If it wasn't, I had a chance but there was no guarantee
that they would even be able to remove the tumour. I was so ill by then
that all I can remember is feeling glad that I was getting a free trip to
Melbourne.'

For eight hours surgeons worked to remove the tumour that had
had such a devastating effect on Louise's life. At one point she stopped
breathing and was saved by an injection directly into the heart. When
the weather turns cold, Louise claims to still be troubled by a sharp
pain in her chest, a permanent legacy of her narrow escape from death.

In the recovery ward, her surgeons delivered the good news first.
She would live and the tumour was benign. The inevitable bad news
that followed was devastating.

'I was blind. I couldn't see anything. The doctors thought I would
probably regain my sight eventually, but that it would take a long time
and it might never return to normal. And, even though they had been
able to remove the entire tumour, they said my recovery would be
slow. It might take years. That wasn't something I had expected at all.'

Within a few months Louise was able to make out grey shadows
and, in time, objects gradually became clearer and more defined. As the
doctors had warned, her rehabilitation was long and not without its

setbacks. She was knocked down by a car early in her recovery period but sustained only minor injuries. As her health improved, she discovered she had lost her sense of smell, a byproduct of the operation. It has never returned.

Also gone was her rabid aggression and illogical behaviour. Her headaches had vanished too and she felt able to think rationally and reasonably for the first time in two years.

'I was back to my old self again, at least mentally. I liked people again, I felt sorry for them ... I wasn't angry all the time. I looked back at those years with the tumour, of the things I said and did and it all seemed like a terrible dream. It was as if it had all happened to someone else, but I know it was me.'

Still only partially sighted, Louise was transferred from Melbourne back to Launceston Hospital. She spent another four months there before finally being deemed well enough for release. For the next two years she would attend hospital regularly for further treatment and rehabilitation. With time came the slow return of her eyesight and a gradual improvement in her general physical health. But the tumour was to have a lasting impact. Louise has never been permitted to drive a car since the operation and has never been able to hold down a full-time job. The lack of support she received from her Launceston friends was not forgotten or forgiven on her return.

'When I got to the stage where I was able to walk around the streets a little, I would meet some of my old friends. They would say, "Oh, we heard about your brain tumour, how terrible." And I would look them in the eye and tell them what I thought of them. I would say, "Last time I saw you cross the street to avoid me. Now you can go jump in the lake." '

The next few years were hard and lonely.

'Those were very lean years for me. I couldn't work, I had no money. Everything I had was from the government — my accommodation, my money, everything. I had enough to survive on and that was all. There was no money for clothes, for wine, for fun. And I had always been a person who loved to laugh, to party, to enjoy myself. It was difficult for me. I was very lucky to be alive, of course; I had no doubts about that. I really believe that all the pills and booze and long hours spent working for the Luftwaffe contributed to my tumour in the first place. So I knew I had had a lucky escape. But still, life was hard and there didn't seem any way out of my situation.'

On the other side of the world, Louise's tragedy was matched by that of her sister Gerda.

'Poor Gerda. Her husband had died some years before and she had taken her two children back to live in Germany. Then, in a fairly short period of time, her son was killed in a car accident and, not long after, her daughter died of leukemia. She was all alone. We talked about getting together; she wanted me to come back to Germany to live with her. But I didn't want to. And she didn't want to come to Australia either. So we couldn't do anything to help each other really. Anyway, I don't think we could have lived together — there were always issues between the two of us and I don't think they would have gone away just because we were older. Gerda was always very strong-willed, she liked to do things her way. She has some funny habits — she likes to stay up half the night and then sleep until noon. We wouldn't have lived well together.'

An article in a local newspaper about Louise's Nazi past opened the door to a brief respite from her despair.

'I got offers to go on TV and of course I took them all. I went on the Mike Walsh Show, the Don Lane Show and I got interviewed by Mike Willessee. They were all quite nice and very friendly to me. I didn't mind answering their questions — it was a bit of fun actually. And of course, they paid me very well and I really needed the money. But it was typical — every time I was on TV, within a few days bills would arrive from the Tax Department or the Social Security — I couldn't win. If I made some money, the government was very quick to take it away from me.'

In 1977, a female friend decided that a good man might just be the cure for Louise's malaise. Taking it upon herself to play matchmaker, she introduced Louise to Ron Johnson, a lanky English builder whose wife had passed away several years before from cancer. It was a spontaneous and mutual attraction.

'I liked him immediately. He was funny and very friendly. He liked to enjoy himself, so we had that in common. As well, he had been a pilot in the war, flying Lancaster bombers. When he told me that, I said, "How could you? Don't you know you were dropping bombs on me?" He just laughed and said, "Honey, if I'd known you were down there, I would have dropped flowers instead".'

Louise and Ron quickly established themselves as a couple, and although Louise maintained her own flat, she spent most of her time living with Ron at his home, about an hour and a half by road from Launceston.

'We enjoyed each other's company very much. He was very generous to me, and after having nothing for so long, I really appreciated that generosity. But he had two sons and neither of them liked me. They resented me, I think. They didn't like the fact that I was a German. And of course, I knew their father's secret and I think that made them uncomfortable.'

Ron Johnson's secret was surprising and not particularly well kept. In fact, the friend who had first introduced them to each other had felt it her duty to warn Louise about it. Ron Johnson was a transvestite.

'Oh, yes, she had told me all about it. Every one of his friends knew. He only kept it a secret from people he didn't think would understand or accept it. His wife had threatened to leave him if he wore women's clothes around the house, and his children were very much against it. But it was something he had to do. I couldn't say I liked it myself; I would have preferred a boyfriend who didn't wear women's underwear and makeup, of course — but I accepted it because it was what he wanted. To me, going out with a man like Ron was another little adventure.'

The first time Ron presented himself to Louise in a dress, high heels and makeup, she burst into laughter.

'He just looked so funny. He was a tall man, a burly man, a builder with big shoulders and big hands. He looked ridiculous really, and his makeup was terrible. He started laughing at my reaction too, and we both knew that this relationship could last because I would accept Ron for what he was.

'He was not effeminate in any way when he was wearing men's clothing. He liked women; he wasn't gay. People often think that transvestites are homosexual but it's not the case. Early on in our time together I went to the library and looked up everything I could about transvestitism. I learned that people are born that way — it's not something that you just choose to do for the sake of it. It's often genetic — and I remember Ron telling me his father used to do the same thing.

'So, I didn't complain about it at all. In fact, I helped him with his hair and makeup all the time — he didn't have much of a clue about things like that — and we would talk about dresses and so on, something we were both really interested in. He had 37 pairs of shoes, you know. He loved shoes. They were all too big for me, unfortunately; otherwise we could have shared a wardrobe!'

Ron Johnson had lived with his predilections all his life. Even the rough and tumble macho world of the Royal Air Force had not prevented him from indulging his obsession with dressing as a woman.

'He told me he would wear a bra and pants under his uniform. Even when he was on duty, flying the plane, he would have women's underwear on the whole time. Can you imagine? I thought that was hilarious.'

While his close friends were supportive, the same could not be said of Launceston society in general.

'Ron always felt very constrained in Launceston. He was forced into being a closet tranny, which he didn't like. He knew he wouldn't be tolerated in Tasmania; there was no way people would accept a man walking around in ladies clothes there. So he liked to go away on holidays to places where he would be understood. He would take me with him. We would go to the Gold Coast. There were special clubs for transvestites, and they would have parties where all the men would dress up and have a great time. They were free to be themselves. Many of them brought their wives and girlfriends along too — so I wasn't the only crazy woman in the world.

'Ron was always happiest when he would dress up and go out in public. He was proud of how he looked and how he felt. Of course, sometimes people were unkind, but too bad for them. He took me to the Melbourne Cup one year and he and some transvestite friends all went fully dressed up. Some young boys on the entry gate saw them and started sniggering and nudging one another. That made me mad. I told them to shut up and mind their own business. It annoyed me that people would make fun of Ron when he was doing nothing to hurt anyone.'

Ron and Louise would be inseparable for the next 20 years. Their only lengthy periods apart came in 1982 and then again in 1995 when Louise travelled back to Europe.

'The first time, my sister paid for me. I spent three months overseas, travelling through Italy, Switzerland and Austria, and of course Germany. It was good to see Gerda again and to see how things had changed. But I didn't feel any urge to stay there. Germany was very different to how I remembered it of course, bigger and much more crowded. Some people were rude, too, and impatient compared to Australians. Before I went on those trips I used to think that moving to Australia was the smartest thing I ever did in my life. After I came back from the first trip in 1982, I knew for sure that I had been right.'

In 1986, Ron and Louise decided to move to the Gold Coast permanently.

'We had always loved it here — the climate, the beaches and the freedom. People were much more understanding of Ron's situation and he could walk around without much bother. I was glad to get away from Launceston; I had grown tired of the cold.'

The couple rented a small flat within walking distance of the ocean and for the next decade lived quietly and contentedly. They joined a local wine club and were both active in local war veterans' associations. Louise took Ron to see plays and concerts and he soon came to share her enthusiasm for music and the arts. There was no talk of marriage as neither saw the necessity. Life for both was simple but idyllic. Even the ever-present tension between Ron's sons — who had also both moved to the Gold Coast — and Louise did little to mar their happiness.

'They still didn't like me; they'd made that clear enough. So, Ron would see them and I would stay behind. I wish it hadn't been like that, but what could I do? It was their problem.'

Then suddenly, it all came to a terrible end. One night Ron suffered a heart attack and was rushed to hospital. His sons arrived soon after and immediately forbade Louise from having any contact with their father. As he lay dying, the woman he had loved for 20 years could do nothing but sit alone in the home they had shared and cry.

'I have never forgiven them for doing that to me. And I never will. We were together for 20 years. He was my Ron. They had no right to punish me like that.'

On the last night of Ron Johnson's life, his children finally relented. They drove Louise to the hospital and allowed her to sit by their father's bedside. By now, Ron had lapsed into a coma. Louise could do nothing more than stroke his arm as he died. The man she called 'the love of her life' was dead at 83 years old.

Today, Louise Fox still lives in the same flat she and Ron shared for so many years. The little girl that grew up by the ocean has returned to it once more, albeit on a vastly different shore. She lives alone these days, but insists she is not lonely. As self-reliant as ever when the situation requires it, Louise keeps herself as active as her health will allow and still relishes an active social life. Her 'little adventures' may be rather more cautious then in days gone by, but she still enjoys experimenting with and experiencing all that life has to offer. She doesn't regret having had no children, despite the companionship they might have provided. 'No, my dear,' she tells me firmly, 'I don't like children really, never have. They are all right when they're small, but teenagers — I don't like them at all. My own childhood was so miserable, too — I suppose I worried that I might turn out to be a mother like mine was. I wouldn't wish that on anybody.'

She remains in regular contact with Gerda, whose own health is now extremely fragile.

'She has a pacemaker and she is not strong. She's as stubborn as ever though and wants to stay living in her own home as long as she can. She still plays the saxophone; she still has that musical gift, just like our father.'

There is another important man in Louise's life these days, although not in a romantic sense. Garry, a fellow German immigrant some thirty years Louise's junior, has become a trusted friend and adviser.

'I first met Garry when Ron was still alive. He ran the wine club we went to. After Ron's death, we ran into each other again and now we look after one another. He helps me out, I help him out. It's good to have someone I can trust and can talk to. Of course, he lives in Toowoomba now, so we only see each other on some weekends. Garry talks about me moving to Toowoomba, but I'm not really interested. I love the Gold Coast and Toowoomba is too cold. But we'll see — I never say never to anything.'

After such a tumultuous life, there is a sense that Louise is now enjoying the amount of time she has to devote to herself. Money remains tight, but there is enough for evenings out with Garry and the occasional bottle or two of wine. Books are her greatest pleasure, however, and she describes a perfect day as one spent reading in bed, eating cake.

'I love to read, I always have. Now, of course, I have more time to do that, which is great. I do the gardening and go shopping and, when my back is up to it, I'll go for a walk along the beach. The cultural life of the Gold Coast is improving too — we have some great shows here now. There is always something on at Jupiter's Casino or the Arts Centre and I go whenever I can. Last year they had Opera in the Park — it was fantastic.'

Age is catching up with Louise, and last year a prolapsed disc left her virtually bed-ridden for months and dependent on home help.

'I had Meals on Wheels, and someone in to do the cleaning and shopping for me. I was very grateful for all that; I couldn't have survived without it.'

Old age does not frighten Louise Fox. For a woman who has seen so much suffering and, in turn, suffered so acutely herself, growing old is of minor concern.

'I think that you need to make the most of every opportunity in life to enjoy yourself and follow your heart. The war taught me that. Grab the good times while you can, before they disappear. I make the most of the time I have left — what's the point of complaining about getting old? Of course, it's not much fun, but what can you do? I feel lucky that I've even got to this age, after all that has happened to me. I should have been dead already, really.'

The insanity of the Nazi years and the deprivations of war have left their mark. A past as turbulent as hers can never truly be outrun or forgotten.

'The biggest impact that those years had on me was to strengthen my backbone. War and suffering are like blows. When they first hit, the pain is terrible. You think you can't survive another one. But when another blow does come, and then, another after that, you learn to deal with it. You get stronger. You resist. And then suddenly, the blows don't hurt so much any more. You learn to cope with them. And during those times when the blows stop altogether — when you are happy and everything is as it should be — then there is nothing to compare with how that makes you feel. You are lighter, freer somehow. And you enjoy that feeling while you can because more blows will come. They always do.'

Painfully aware of the futility of war, Louise is equally certain of its inevitability. A keen student of history, she is adamant that mankind will cease fighting only when there is no one left to fight.

'You read any history book — it doesn't matter whether you are talking about the ancient Assyrians or modern history. There were always wars and they were always pointless. People always died for nothing and countries were destroyed. It has never stopped in the whole history of man — and it will not, in my opinion. That is the tragedy, but also the truth.'

Those same history books, she maintains, have judged the German people and their role in the war unfairly.

'People will say that the German people wanted the war, that they knew about the Jews being killed, that they wanted all these terrible things to happen. That is just not true. There was nothing special or different about the German people that made them more likely to have a war than any other people in Europe. Hitler was the difference. Hitler was the cause of it all. Any nation in Europe that found itself controlled by him would have reacted in the same way. If Hitler had been British, the British might now be blamed for the Holocaust. Who knows? But I can say from my heart that we were victims of the Nazis too.'

As for how history will judge the part she herself played, Louise is adamant that her conscience is clear.

'For those people who would condemn me, who would say I should have done this or done that, I would say to them — feel happy that you were not in my shoes. Be thankful that you did not have to make the choices I was forced to make. Be glad you were not born in Germany during the reign of Adolf Hitler.'

Although she dislikes the notion that she is in some ways a child of the Third Reich, Louise admits that the intense propaganda of the Nazi era had an impact on every German, particularly the young and impressionable like herself.

'Of course, it would be impossible to say that I could have been surrounded by all this brainwashing and not be influenced by it in some ways. I admired Goering for a time, and even Hitler. I thought Goebbels was an impressive orator. I admired the discipline of my Hitler Youth meetings and the patriotism that became a part of our lives just prior to the war and during the early years of the conflict. Perhaps those feelings are a result of propaganda, I can't really say. It's just how I feel. But all the propaganda in the world couldn't make me hate the Jews or believe that the concentration camps were a good thing. No form of brainwashing can change your basic morality. Hitler gave Germans a reason to feel good about themselves again, a reason to hope that one day we would be a strong country again. There was nothing wrong with that. However, what was wrong was that he went mad with power and took us down the wrong path. What started as noble intentions, perhaps, ended up as a tragedy for everyone. But I cannot blame Germany or the Germans for what happened. I blame only Hitler and his admirers.'

Several years ago, Louise was attending a concert with friends. Enjoying the pleasures of an orchestra in fine form, Louise was not expecting the sudden clash of cymbals required by the score. Before she even knew what was happening, she was huddled on the floor of the concert hall, head down, bracing herself for a bombing raid that would never come.

'I couldn't believe I had done it. I was very embarrassed. Just for a moment, I had forgotten where I was. The noise startled me, and I reverted to instinct. I guess some part of me is still on the alert, still prepared for danger.'

Wars may end, tyrants may be defeated. But for those who have experienced the cruelties of both, life can never again be as it was. An ordinary woman who survived the most extraordinary of times, Louise Fox's most valuable legacy may well be to remind us all of that fact.

NOTES

CHAPTER 1:

1. Carl Zuckmeyer, *Als wär sein Stück von mir*, 1966, pp. 311-14, reprinted as *A Part of Myself* (translated by Richard and Clara Winston), Harcourt Brace Jovanovich, New York, 1970, p. 217.

2. David Hudson, 'Where the horror came from', www.greencine.com, January 2005.

3. 'The Western Front', *War Times Journal*, www.richtofen.com/ww1/sum/, 2003.

4. Anthony Read, *The Devil's Disciples*, Pimlico Books, London, 2004, p. 16.

5. Adolf Hitler, *Mein Kampf*, Houghton Mifflin Books, pp.204-6.

6. Ibid., p 103.

7. Professor Gerhard Rempel, 'The Weimar Republic 1: Economic and Political Problems',

    http://mars.acnet.wnec.edu/~grempel/courses/germany/lectures/20weimar1.html.

8. Illustrated London News Picture Library. Cat. reference number ZPER 34/154.

9. Doug Bandow, 'American's Forgotten War', www.cato.org/dailys/12-21-98.htm, Cato Institute, 1998.

10. Gordon Craig, *Germany 1866-1945*, Oxford Paperbacks, 1980.

11. Ibid.

12. Konrad Heiden, *Der Fuehrer: Hitler's Rise to Power*, Houghton Mifflin,1944.

13. *New York Times* (archives), 30 October 1923.

14. Edwin L James, 'Failure of the revolt halts Paris plans', *New York Times*, 10 November 1923.

15. Hanseatic League: www.economicexpert.com/a/.HanseaticLeague.html.

16. The Weimar Republic: www.historyhome.co.uk/europe/weimar.htm.

17. Richard J. Evans, *The Coming of the Third Reich*, Penguin Books, London, 2004, p. 260.

CHAPTER 2:

1. William Shirer, *The Rise and Fall of the Third Reich*, Touchstone Books, New York, 1988, p 256.

2. Mary Mills, 'Propaganda and Children During the Hitler Years', www.jewishvirtuallibrary.org/jsource/Holocaust/propchill.html, 2005.

3. Werner May, *Deutscher National-Katechismus*, second edition, Breslau: Verlag von Heinrich Handel, 1934, pp. 22-6.

4. Nazi Germany and Education: www.historylearningsite.co.uk, 2002.

5. Gilmer W. Blackburn, 'The portrayal of Christianity in the history textbooks of Nazi Germany', in *Church History*, Vol 49, 1980, p. 155.

6. Anthony Read, *The Devil's Disciples*, Pimlico Books, London, 2004, p.180.

7. Mary Mills, op. cit.

8. Werner May, op. cit.

9. Elwira Bauer, *Trau keinem Fuchs auf grüner Heid und keinem Jud auf seinem Eid*, Sturmer Verlag, Nuremberg, 1936.

10. Anthony Read, op. cit., p.301.

11. Richard J. Evans, *The Coming of the Third Reich*, Penguin Books, London, 2004, p. 389.

12. David Welch, *Propaganda and the German Cinema 1933-1945*, revised edition, I.B. Tauris Publishers, London, 2001, p. 46.

13. Anthony Read, op. cit, p. 441.

14. George Orwell, 'Anti-Semitism in Britain', *England, Your England and Other Essays*, Secker and Warburg, London, 1953, p.169.

15. Anthony Read, op. cit., p. 508.

16. Report by Hugh Carleton Greene, *Daily Telegraph*, London, 10 November 1938.

17. Anthony Read, op. cit., p.515.

18. Rafael Medoff, 'Kristallnacht and the World's Response', *Jewish Weekly*, New York, November 2003.

19. Adolf Hitler, *Mein Kampf*, Houghton Mifflin Books, p. 347.

20. The Hitler Youth: www.historylearningsite.co.uk/hitler_youth.htm, 2002.

21. Richard Grunberger, *A Social History of the Third Reich,* Penguin Books, 1991.

22. John Simkin, 'The German Girls' League',
www.spartacusschoolnet.co.uk/2wwgirls.htm.

23. The Avalon Project: Collected Proceedings of the Nuremberg Trials,
www.yale.edu/lawweb/avalon/imt/proc/judfritz.htm.

24. William J. Shirer, *The Nightmare Years,* Birlinn Publishers, 2002, pp.198-9.

CHAPTER 3:

1. 'Starvation over Europe (Made in Germany): A Documented Record 1943',
Institute of Jewish Affairs, New York, 1943, pp 37, 47, 52.

2. Ibid.

3. Joseph Goebbels, 'England's Guilt', *Illustrierter Beobachter*, 1939, p. 14.

4. Richard Overy, *Goering*, Barnes & Noble, New York, 2003, p. 77.

5. Ibid., p. 78.

6. 'The Army Enslaved': www.joric.com/conspiracy/enslaved.htm.

7. 'Recipes of Wartime Europe': http://timewitnesses.org/english/food/index.html.

8. Joseph Goebbels, 'An Open Discussion', *Das Eherne Herz*, Zentralverlag der
NSDAP, Munich, 1943.

CHAPTER 4:

1. Anthony Read, *The Devil's Disciples*, Pimlico Books. London, 2004, p. 720.

2. Rudolf Hess, speech entitled 'The Oath to Hitler', first reprinted in *Reden,*
Zentralverlag der NSDAP, Munich, 1938, pp. 10-14.

3. Joseph Goebbels, *The Early Goebbels Diaries*, Praeger, Germany, 1963, p. 15.4.
Anthony Read, op. cit., p. 67.

5. Erich Gritzbach, *Hermann Göring: The Man and his Works*, Hurst and Blackett,
1939, p. 22.

6. Douglas M. Kelley, *22 Cells in Nuremberg,* W.H. Allen, 1947.

7. Henrik Eberle and Uhl, Matthias, *The Hitler Book: The secret dossier prepared for
Stalin*, John Murray, London, 2005.

8. Richard Overy, *Goering*, Barnes & Noble, New York, 2003, p.171.

9. Adolf Hitler, *Mein Kampf*, Houghton Mifflin Books, p. 241.

10. Albert Speer, *Inside the Third Reich*, Sphere, 1983, p. 644.

11. 'The Bombing of Germany': www.historylearningsite.co.uk/bombing.htm.

12. Ibid.

13. 'Indiscriminate Bombings': www.valourandhorror.com/BC/issues/Indiscr1.php.

14. Anthony Read, op. cit., photograph no. 22.

CHAPTER 5:

1. http://en.wikipedia.org/wiki/Oradour-sur-Glane.

2. 'The Fire Bombing of Dresden: an eyewitness account',
    http://timewitnesses.org/english/~lothar.html.

3. 'The Fall of Berlin, 1945', http://eyewitnesstohistory.com/berlin.htm.

4. 'The Death of Hitler',
    http://www.historyplace.com/worldwar2/timeline/death.htm.

5. Ibid.

6. Anthony Read, *The Devil's Disciples*, Pimlico Books, London, 2004, p. 918.

CHAPTER 6:

1. 1. Norbert Trippen, *Josef Kardinal Frings (1887-1978), Volume 1: Sein Wirken für das Erzbistum Köln und für die Kirche in Deutschland*. Verffentlichungen der Kommission für Zeitgeschichte. Ferdinand Schugh, Paderborn, 2003, http://www.h-net.org/reviews/showrev.cgi?path=219831127322357.

2. http://www.globalsecurity.org/military/library/report/other/us-army_germany_1944-46_ch07.htm.

3. S. Jonathan Wiesen, *The Work of Memory*, University of Illinois Press ebook, www.press.uillinois.edu/epub/books/confino/ch9.html.

4. Daniel J. Goldhagen, *Hitler's Willing Executioners: Ordinary Germans and the Holocaust*, Random House, New York, 1996, p. 203.

5.   'The Avalon Project – Nuremberg Trial Proceedings', Vol. 1,
     www.yale.edu/lawweb/avalon/imt/proc/vl-08.htm.

6.   Ibid.

7.   'House of Wannsee Conference',
     http://www.ghwk.de/engl/catalog/cateng14.htm.

BIBLIOGRAPHY

Books:

Bauer, Elwira, *Trau keinem Fuchs auf grüner Heid und keinem Jud auf seinem Eid*, Sturmer Verlag, Nuremberg, 1936.

Craig, Gordon, *Germany 1866-1945*, Oxford Paperbacks, 1980.

Eberle, Henrik and Uhl, Matthias, *The Hitler Book: The secret dossier prepared for Stalin*, John Murray, London, 2005.

Evans, Richard J., *The Coming of the Third Reich*, Penguin Books, London, 2004.

Goebbels, Joseph, *The Early Goebbels Diaries*, Praeger, Germany, 1963.

Goldhagen, Daniel J., *Hitler's Willing Executioners: Ordinary Germans and the Holocaust*, Random House, New York, 1996.

Gritzbach, Erich, *Hermann Goering: The Man and his Works*, Hurst and Blackett, 1939.

Grunberger, Richard, *A Social History of the Third Reich*, Penguin Books, 1991.

Hayden, Deborah, *Pox: Genius, Madness and the Mysteries of Syphilis*, Basic Books, New York, 2003.

Heiden, Konrad, *Der Führer: Hitler's Rise to Power*, Houghton Mifflin, 1944.

Hitler, Adolf, *Mein Kampf*, Houghton Mifflin Books.

Kelley, Douglas M., *22 Cells in Nuremberg*, W.H Allen, 1947.

May, Werner, *Deutscher National-Katechismus*, second edition, Breslau: Verlag von Heinrich Handel, 1934.

Orwell, George, *England, Your England and Other Essays*, Secker and Warburg, London, 1953.

Overy, Richard, *Goering*, Barnes & Noble, New York, 2003.

Read, Anthony, *The Devil's Disciples*, Pimlico Books, London, 2004.

Shirer, William J., *The Rise and Fall of the Third Reich*, Touchstone Books, New York, 1988.

Shirer, William J., *The Nightmare Years*, Birlinn Publishers, 2002.

Speer, Albert, *Inside the Third Reich*, Sphere, 1983.

Welch, David, *Propaganda and the German Cinema 1933-1945*, revised edition, I.B. Tauris Publishers, London, 2001.

Zuckmeyer, Carl, *Als wär sein Stück von mir* (1966), reprinted as *A Part of Myself* (translated by Richard and Clara Winston), Harcourt Brace Jovanovich, New York, 1970.

Articles:

Blackburn, Gilmer W., 'The portrayal of Christianity in the history textbooks of Nazi Germany', *Church History*, Vol. 49, 1980.

Goebbels, Joseph, 'England's Guilt', *Illustrierter Beobachter*, 1939.

Goebbels, Joseph, 'An Open Discussion', *Das Eherne Herz*, Zentralverlag der NSDAP, Munich, 1943.

Greene, Hugh Carleton, *Daily Telegraph*, London, 10 November 1938.

Hess, Rudolf, 'The Oath to Hitler' (speech), reprinted in *Reden*, Zentralverlag der NSDAP, Munich, 1938.

James, Edwin L., 'Failure of the revolt halts Paris plans', *New York Times*, 10 November 1923.

Medoff, Rafael, 'Kristallnacht and the World's Response', *Jewish Weekly*, New York, November 2003.

'Starvation over Europe (Made in Germany): A Documented Record 1943', Institute of Jewish Affairs, New York, 1943.

New York Times (archives).

Websites:

www.cato.org/dailys

www.economicexpert.com

http://www.ghwk.de/engl/catalog/cateng14.htm

http://www.globalsecurity.org/military/library/report/other/us-army_germany_1944-46_ch07.htm

www.greencine.com

www.historyhome.co.uk/europe/weimar.htm

www.historylearningsite.co.uk

http://www.historyplace.com/worldwar2/timeline/death.htm

http://www.h-net.org/reviews/showrev.cgi?path=219831127322357

www.jewishvirtuallibrary.org

www.joric.com/conspiracy/enslaved.htm

http://mars.acnet.wnec.edu/~grempel/courses/germany/lectures/20weimar1.html

http://www.press.uillinois.edu/epub/books/confino/ch9.html

www.richtofen.com

www.spartacusschoolnet.co.uk/2wwgirls.htm

http://timewitnesses.org/english

www.valourandhorror.com

http://en.wikipedia.org/wiki/Oradour-sur-Glane

www.yale.edu/lawweb/avalon/

Exisle Publishing is proud to introduce the Hourglass series. Hourglass books feature the true stories of ordinary women who have lived extraordinary lives. They are as varied as the women who love reading them, from the passionate and heart-wrenching to the humorous and uplifting, and range widely across continents and lifestyles. But they have one thing in common: they are all superb stories offering great reading.

Also available in this series:

THE GIRL WITH THE CARDBOARD PORT
Judith L. McNeil

Judith McNeil has lived a life that few of us can begin to imagine. She has faced tragedy and heartache, experienced crippling poverty and hunger and suffered unforgivable violence. But she has emerged a survivor, a woman with an indomitable will and the courage and resourcefulness to forge a new life for herself against all odds.

The death of Judy's father in a railway accident when she is only fourteen triggers a chain of events that will lead her first to the slums of Sydney and ultimately to far-flung Singapore and Malaya. Here, she finds friendship in the company of an Indian servant, love in the arms of a jungle warrior and hope in the laughter of her children.

Set against the backdrop of the political upheaval and widespread racial violence that swept through Singapore and Malaya in the early 1960s, *The Girl with the Cardboard Port* takes you into a world that few Europeans would have encountered. From glittering society balls to the isolation of a Malay kampong, from riches to poverty, Judy experiences a world of contrasts, often living in fear for her life and those of her children. And through it all, she has only one dream: to return home to Australia.

Raw and compelling, her story will linger in your mind long after the final page.

ISBN 0 908988 80 X

HOURGLASS

To be on the mailing list to receive further information about the Hourglass series, please write to **Hourglass, c/o Moonrising, Narone Creek Road, Wollombi, NSW 2325, Australia** or to **P.O. Box 60-490, Titirangi, Auckland 1230, New Zealand.**